D1536960

FREE INDEED

FROM

SORCERY BONDAGE

A Proven Scriptural Ministry

Marvin S. Wolford

So if the Son sets you free,
you will be free indeed.
—John 8:36

ISBN: 0-9670915-0-0

Library of Congress Number: 99-093720

Copyright © 1999 by Marvin S. Wolford

Printed by Pathway Press

Printed in the United States
of America

Dedicated to
my precious wife

Jean

Whose constant help
made this possible

BIOGRAPHICAL INFORMATION

Rev. Dr. Marvin S. Wolford has 42 years of experience ministering in the Republic of Congo as a United Methodist missionary. Converted and called into the ministry while serving as an agricultural missionary in 1957, Dr. Wolford co-founded the Kafakumba Pastors' School which has grown from 6 to 125 pastors. Teaching pastors and evangelism/church planting convinced both Marvin and his wife, Jean, that a vital Holy Spirit led church is impossible without the Scriptures. In 1966 they began, along with Congolese pastors, the first translation of the Old Testament and a re-translation of the New Testament in the Uruund language. The N.T. has been published by the United Bible Societies, and the O.T. is ready to be typeset as this book goes to press.

The Bible translation led to a focus on the sorcery problem facing the Church in Congo. When war drove them from Kapanga, Dr. Wolford completed his Doctor of Missiology degree at Trinity Evangelical Divinity School in Deerfield, IL. Research for that degree led to this volume which has been taught to African Methodist pastors, Pentecostal pastors, missionaries and Congolese, and every 3 years at the Nairobi Evangelical Graduate School of Theology. Students have been from the countries of West, Central, and East Africa, and without exception they declare, "This is our problem; this is where we live!"

Dr. Wolford also has a Bachelor of Science degree in Agriculture Education from the University of Illinois, and a Master of Theology from Candler School of Theology at Emory University in Atlanta, GA. which included biblical and theological studies at Asbury Theological Seminary.

His wife, Jean, has been secretary/computer person for all of their Bible translation, teaching and publishing experiences. At this time they are preparing to return to their ministries in Congo. They have three sons, Thomas, Stephen and Andrew. Thomas and Stephen are serving as pilots in Africa and Andrew has volunteered there as well.

INTRODUCTION

Paths crisscross every corner of Africa and provide routes to countless destinations. Once while walking on a path in Congo, which had been shown to us by a local resident in an area with which we were familiar, my wife, Jean, and I became quite lost. A friend had pointed out the wrong path which led to the wrong destination. Just at dark we cut through gardens and tall elephant grass and found the right path to lead us home.

People following the paths of sorcery, which were shown to them by family and friends, are desperately lost. Many have a hunger to be finished with sorcery and to find the path to freedom, but few have found The Path so beautifully provided by God!

"What does God say about sorcery? It is the most serious problem in the Church today." Ordained pastors who had been trained in the most prestigious seminary in Southern Congo asked me this question in 1976.

Two important points were made that day. First, sorcery is a modern, up-to-date problem of enormous magnitude. Second, pastors are unprepared to minister to the problem. There are exceptions, but extensive research indicates that these pastors are not isolated in their quest for a meaningful ministry to sorcery-bound people in their churches. Bishops, national church leaders—both lay and clergy—as well as members of the local churches, all indicate that this is a very ecumenical problem that extends beyond national borders.

While teaching several seminars at the Nairobi Evangelical Graduate School of Theology in Nairobi, Kenya, I have had the privilege of sharing with students from many of the nations across central Africa. All of these students were well educated and keenly perceptive Christians, and they extended the perimeters of the sorcery problem to include their home country, their tribe, and their families. One student in 1993 in response to the sorcery lessons said, "This is life for us; this is where we live." Experience reveals that this "life" is the same whether in the cities or in the remote bush areas. The variations are, of course, endless, but the same central sorcery theme is universal and, likewise, able to be treated Biblically.

Unfortunately, few missionaries have understood the problem.

Many have ministered in the name of Jesus Christ and in the power of the Holy Spirit and missed grasping this problem. When the above question was handed to me in a letter, I laughed. "How could I possibly speak to the sorcery problem—I know nothing about it," was my immediate response. As an ordained missionary, I was obviously unaware of the problem.

Western missionaries have easily included sorcery with superstition on a shallow—"don't bother me and I won't bother you"—basis. For most westerners, it seems, leading people to make a decision to accept Jesus Christ as their Saviour, plus some Bible teaching, is adequate. Few have had any comparable experience in sorcery and, historically, missionaries have even denied the existence of sorcery. For the few who believed that it constituted a problem, they had no cultural framework for comprehending the ubiquitousness of sorcery. There isn't anything else like it. Little, short of terminal cancer, is comparable!

This ministry addresses both the problem as it exists today, and the solution as it has existed since the Cross. Often this includes the obvious, but the obvious must be seen in the context of sorcery-bound peoples. Even trite Christian applications are presented without apology, because for someone it may not be trite—and even the trite, when based on God's Word, can be profound in ministry.

There is no attempt to be definitive, but every attempt has been made to open an understanding of problems that will make possible further openings in other local settings. No lessons or sermon outlines are included lest this limit or prejudice some readers. It is far better for Christians to take this raw material and, using the suggestions found here, to develop their own locally pertinent responses. There is, of course, no end to the light given by the Scriptures, so what is presented here is intended to begin a process of contextualization that will make them vivid, pertinent, and totally practical wherever this ministry is undertaken.

May this be an open door to introduce many to the gross problem facing the Christian churches and the glorious, victorious solution offered by God himself in his Word.

Marvin S. Wolford
Missionary to the Republic of Congo

TABLE OF CONTENTS

PART I

SORCERY BONDAGE
IN FOCUS

1

THE TRADITIONAL CONTEXT OF SORCERY

The patient was seriously ill. As the doctor examined him at the Samuteb mission hospital it became obvious that surgery was necessary. Also obvious to the doctor was the anemic condition of the patient. Good food with protein and vitamins was prescribed for one month—hopefully, this would provide strength to survive the required surgery. The patient departed deeply worried and fearful. Obviously, he thought, the doctor had discovered evil spirits inside his body with the x-ray machine. He must be afraid to operate as long as the spirits remained—thus the one month delay.

Yav was 5 years old. His hair was mostly straight and rusty colored instead of black and curly. His stomach was grossly distended as it hung on an emaciated body. His problem was kwashiorkor, the malnutrition disease that leads to death unless treated with an adequate diet. But Yav had a friend. A missionary lady found him before it was too late, and with daily "doses" of high protein food she nursed him out of the crisis. However, his friend returned to her country, and Yav died not many weeks later. He died because his parents believed (along with others in their culture) that kwashiorkor is caused by sorcerers who "fish" the life out of children to kill them. He was marked for death, they believed, therefore, no effort on their part could save him.

Makal and her husband were deeply worried. After eight years of marriage they didn't have even one child. They were happy together, but her parents were insisting that she go to a sorcerer to get "birth power." Likewise, her husband's parents knew just the person to sell her "medicine" to open her womb for childbirth. The distress, the worry, and the fear from the pressures came from the basic belief that all barrenness is caused by sorcery power. More powerful "power," the family reasoned, would produce the required children.

Twelve year old Kaleng had suffered much from the huge open ulcers on his body. The sores had deformed one hand and stopped movement of one elbow. When brought to a Christian dispensary by his grandmother Kaleng had five open wounds two and three inches in diameter. With supplementary diet and twice daily treatments the hideous progress was reversed. Health and healing were definitely within his grasp. However, one day Kaleng's father arrived and forceably took him back to their village, and certain death. No treatment, he explained, could cure Kaleng because his illness was caused by his grandmother through sorcery.

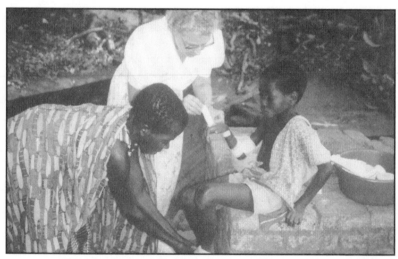

Sorcery beliefs caused the death of this recovering boy in Kafakumba, Congo

These true stories illustrate that virtually all animistic peoples are sorcery-bound. They are helplessly in its grasp. Sorcery is not an independent phenomenon among animistic peoples. Other related activities co-exist with sorcery, and, in fact, are almost indistinguishable from it. However, sorcery must be recognized as the primary limiting factor in their lives and culture. People relate to the economic, political, social, and religious aspects of their society; however, nothing permeates the entire culture as sorcery does. It is omnipresent, thus influencing all important decisions. Animistic people believe that every act of every day of every life is affected by the spiritual aspects of everything involved in the act, good or bad. Workmen, hunters, housewives, students—all are influenced by these beliefs. Rare exceptions do exist, but to understand the problem one must realize the hold that the beliefs in sorcery have on families, clans, and tribes all across many cultures.

Bishop Ngoi Wakadilo of the Republic of Congo speaks of the traditional beliefs held by the Luba people of north central Shaba province. He notes: "...a person is related spiritually to all of which he is a part. It is like that with his house, his shoes, his clothes, and all he contacts."[1] It is this basic realm of living spirits as well as the spiritual relationships with people that provide the vehicle for sorcery.

The details of sorcery, as practiced by many different tribes or peoples, provide endless variety. Likewise, within any one tribe or clan there may be many differences in these practices. However, animistic peoples are unified in the basic belief that sorcery exists. The detailed differences are not as important as the universal fact that sorcery is embraced by virtually everyone. It is the most powerful influence in their cultures.

Animism

Each culture is unique; therefore, terminology which quite adequately expresses the life of one people may be quite misleading when describing another people, similar though they may seem to be. However, valid terms will be borrowed and new terms introduced as we make these observations.

Animism is a term whose meaning includes:

1. The doctrine that all life is produced by a spiritual force separate from matter

2. The belief that all natural phenomena have souls independent of their physical being

3. A belief in the existence of spirits, demons, etc.[2] Thus animists will refer to a rock formation as living, or they regard lightning as an obedient servant, or react to disease as if it were sent personally via some spirit.

One needs to be more precise, however, for many regions have a modified animism. For them it is not the case that all natural phenomena, such as the rock formation and the lightning mentioned above, are regarded as having souls, though a spiritual power certainly attends everything. This spiritual power is a form of life, but it stops short of having a soul—that which can will to do something or determine the morality of its own actions.

Dynamism

Edwin W. Smith, in his book about the culture of the Ila people, refers to this type of religion as "dynamism." He describes this as: "The belief in, the practice associated with the belief in hidden, mysterious, super-sensible, pervading energy, powers, potencies, forces."[3] There is no mention of living spirits and forces in this description, so this would seem to be an incomplete statement of the beliefs held by animists.

Therefore, modified animism, which deletes the soul of animism and injects life to dynamism, seems to be a more accurate term.

John Mbiti, an African theologian and author, does not accept the use of either term. In describing the Ashanti's tribal religion in west Africa, however, he says that they "have spirits that animate trees, rivers, animals, charms and the like...." Also, in a list of possibilities he includes "...power to make inanimate objects turn into biologically living creatures...."[4]

Perhaps Mbiti is not justified in rejecting these basic terms without providing an alternate. Perhaps the concept of modified animism mentioned above expresses his observations as well.

Modified Animism Illustrated

For example, during the 1960's there was a demonstration by local people in Kafakumba, in Congo's Shaba province, of how to smelt iron. First a container for charcoal and iron bearing pebbles was fashioned out of clay in the form of a squatting woman. It was about six feet tall and had a diameter of about four feet at the top. Fire was then forced up through this clay container by home-made bellows made out of animal skins, while chants were sung by the men who were operating the bellows. When one of them became exhausted, another took his place, always without missing one beat on the bellows' sticks. This rhythmic work was always accompanied by chants. The workers kept this up for an entire day and night. When the mixture was heated to the right temperature, the clay woman supposedly "gave birth" to the molten iron. One could ask, Was there a soul or just a spiritual power in the rocks? Was the woman to whom they chanted a soul or a living spirit? Did the fire have a soul, or was it just a force being used?

The figure, shaped like a woman, indicates that more than the forces of dynamism were involved. However, the immediate abandonment of the figure following the completion of the task, and the use of the smelted iron for menial tasks, indicate that less than the soul of pure animism was intended. Even though some of these questions must go unanswered, a modified animism seems to be the most reasonable description of the beliefs of the Kafakumba people. This includes a living spiritual power that has no soul.

It is difficult to know whether this belief in animism preceded sorcery or if sorcery preceded animism. However, since we are here concerned with the problems which these people are now facing, we will assume that a modified animism is the background for the practice of sorcery. One could also say that this animism is the soil from which sorcery sprouts and thrives. This is illustrated in the language of the Aruund people of western Shaba in Congo. One of their nine noun classes is a personal class which includes not only human beings and animals, but the sun, moon and some other natural forces as well. Many objects considered inanimate to the outsider are considered to be living forces with spirits to the Aruund.

Magic

It is evident that there is some connection between animism and the practices of magic, witchcraft, and sorcery. These terms are not precise and often overlap, however, some differences are notable.

Magic is an intermediate general term which clarifies how the background of animism relates to sorcery. Animistic beliefs provide for the spiritual realm, but "magic is the technique of manipulating supernatural or supernormal forces to attain one's own ends."[5] Many of the people believe in these invisible forces and carry these beliefs with them into the village and the market place. In the absence of scientific explanations of disease and misfortune, they turn to the various forms of magic for help. At other times certain definite measures are taken to ward off the evil powers. The spirits are exorcised or driven away as much as possible in an effort to give protection from evil. Magic is also used to try to bring success and to heal the sick.

In a land where misfortune is never far away and where any success is a very difficult process, magic becomes everyone's constant companion. From an early age they are always motivated to seek control of the invisible forces. In fact, "Children are told that sorcerers go about naked and kill other people."[6] No part of life is exempt from the necessity of interacting with the immediate spiritual realm. This is attempted through magic of various forms.

E. E. Evans-Pritchard writes of the Zande people in northeastern Congo as follows:

> Witchcraft is ubiquitous. It plays its part in every activity of Zande life; in agriculture, fishing, hunting pursuits; in domestic life of homesteads as well as in the communal life of the district and court; it is an important theme of mental life in which it forms the background of a vast panorama of oracles and magic; its influence is plainly stamped on law and morals, etiquette and religion; it is prominent in technology and language; there is no niche or corner of Zande culture into which it does not twist itself.[7]

As stated in the definition above, magic is the technique of manipulating supernatural or supernormal forces to attain one's own ends, good or evil. Without an absolute Good or an absolute Evil, the user of magic is set loose on a sea of possibilities with only the rudder of selfishness to guide him. Writing about African magic in general, E. Idowu defines the motto of magic: "My will be done."[8] The user of magic is interested in abating the forces that would cause him ill health or bad luck in any area of life. He also wants desperately to augment his chances for receiving any benefit from any favorable forces. Since there is no absolute evaluation of good or evil, then whatever one considers to be for his own best interest may cause misfortune or even death for someone else. It is precisely at this point that this whole idea of magic needs further clarification.

Westerners use the terms "white" magic and "black" magic. "White" or "good" magic describes the supposed positive or constructive manipulation of the invisible forces. It also identifies and neutralizes the evil magician.

Black magic, in contrast to white magic, is magic practiced with evil intent. Its purpose may be to bring illness, misfortune, or even death. It must be noted here that to users of any magic the good or evil is relative to the user and the conditions. In other words,

The Relationship of Sorcery to the Supernatural Realms

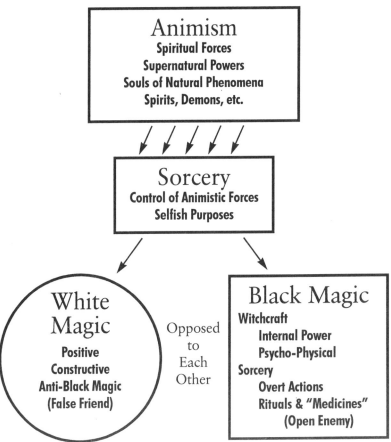

Animism
Spiritual Forces
Supernatural Powers
Souls of Natural Phenomena
Spirits, Demons, etc.

Sorcery
Control of Animistic Forces
Selfish Purposes

White Magic
Positive
Constructive
Anti-Black Magic
(False Friend)

Opposed
to
Each
Other

Black Magic
Witchcraft
 Internal Power
 Psycho-Physical
Sorcery
 Overt Actions
 Rituals & "Medicines"
 (Open Enemy)

the moral evaluation of magic will be changed by the user to suit his needs.

Witchcraft

The Azande of northeastern Congo differentiate between witchcraft and sorcery, but both terms are considered forms of black magic.

To them, the difference between a sorcerer and a witch is that the former uses the techniques of magic and derives his power from "medicines," while the latter acts without rites and spells and uses hereditary psycho-physical powers to attain his ends. Both alike are enemies of men, and Azande class them together. Witchcraft and sorcery are opposed to, and opposed by good magic.[9]

John Middleton and E. H. Winter report on a similar situation in East Africa. They note that in that area: "Witchcraft...is a part of an individual's being, a part of his innermost self, while sorcery is merely a technique which a person utilizes."[10] This means that the power of witchcraft is within the witch (In Africa witches are not necessarily women). Some Africans believe this power resides in the small intestine of witches and does not depend on overt activities for its continued potency. Their activities center around invisible spiritual forces. On the other hand, the sorcerer's technique may involve not only spiritual forces but also certain "medicines" made from secret recipes, and/or the use of rituals or other special activities. In certain areas of Uganda, for example, the father inserts the sorcery "medicine" into the rectum of his child. This insures that certain spirit forces will be present as the child grows to become a sorcerer.

Sorcery—All Inclusive

In southern Congo sorcery and witchcraft are both "enemies of man" and they "class them together," as the Azande to the northeast do. There are linguistic reasons for this. For example, the French language classifies these two concepts together. Black magic, *magie noire*, is considered the same as sorcery, *sorcellerie*. Likewise, the Aruund people of southwestern Congo use one word that covers the activities of both the witch and the sorcerer. That general term is *ulaj*, and the practitioner, whether male or female, is called the *mulaj*. Sorcery, then, is a justifiably inclusive term in the context of animism.

Sorcery among the Aruund

Rev. Nshid Sampas of Shaba province explains the meaning of *ulaj*. In an interview he helped to illuminate the two characteristics of black magic included in this term by the Aruund people. At one point Sampas described witchcraft as used by the older people.

It is almost always a verbal thing. If they curse someone and say that that person is going to die or get sick, and if another party hears the curse and observes when sickness comes to the other person, then the other party may go and tell the old person that indeed sickness came as he had called for; thus that old person is identified with sorcery from then on. Note that no poisons or physical contact are used.[11]

In this case *ulaj* represents witchcraft, since there is no use of tangible items or physical contact. This agrees with Sampas' earlier statement that *ulaj* is a spiritual power that does not use material objects. Later, however, he adjusted that somewhat and added the concept of sorcery, which uses a combination of spiritual power and physical objects. He stated: "Actually they can employ some 'medicines' or poisons if the curse or spiritual power does not take effect."[12] This is illustrated by describing the use of a vine as a cause of death, in case a curse fails to do so. A piece of vine is placed on the path where the victim will pass by. Only the sorcerer sees that the vine is a snake which is capable of causing death. When the victim comes along the path, the "snake" bites and kills him. For the Aruund then, *ulaj* includes spiritual powers, as well as tangible objects used in combination with spiritual power. There is no type of black magic or witchcraft which is not covered by this term.

Sorcery among the Luba

Mukalay wa Ngoi, a converted sorcerer from the Luba people of south central Congo, also employs one term for both witchcraft and sorcery. The Luba term for sorcery is *bufwishi*, and it is very similar to *ulaj* as used by the Aruund people. He says:

A sorcerer can become invisible to ordinary people. The spirits of the people he has killed—these can make him

Bark from this tree provides poison for sorcery "medicine" in Congo.

invisible. Sorcery has to do with the spirit and moves like the wind into a house.[13]

In this illustration only the spirits of the deceased are referred to. The spirit realm was very real to Mukalay. For example, he often went to graveyards and, according to him, spoke with the deceased. Later he claims to have used these spirits to work for him in sorcery. They could be sent out to harm other people according to his instructions. Thus these spirits enhanced his sorcery power. This explains one of the meanings of *bufwishi*.

Bufwishi also includes another type of sorcery that involves objects such as "medicines" and poisons. This is illustrated by Mukalay's search for the power to control lightning. He was told by his grandfather, an elder sorcerer, that a certain "medicine" was necessary to obtain this power. The "medicine," in this case, would be used to gain control of the spirits of the lightning. The elder sorcerer instructed Mukalay to bring him an interesting list of ingredients for the "medicine." He lists them as:

> 8 needles (or 4); a piece of a bridge pole; a small stone from the river where people bathe; the branch of a tree that fell in the wind but did not touch the ground; the tail and the nose of a rat; a small mat woven by his own wife; the red feathers of a special bird; a snail; a palm tree blossom; gunpowder; blood from a chicken whose head was severed with one blow only; and whiskey.[14]

We must listen to Mukalay's account of the results to get the proper perspective:

Grandfather drank a little bit of the whiskey and put a small amount of 'medicine' in the snail shell. Then he told me, 'We will send lightning three times today, if God is willing' [an expression only]. Then he took the needles and put them in the snail; he put some gunpowder in too, and lit it with a match. We heard a terribly loud report like a gun being fired. He did this three times, and all three times it sounded the same. Then he told me that all three bolts of lightning would strike a tree that stood by the door of the house. And sure enough, all three bolts struck that tree, and to this day it is completely dead.[15]

Thus Mukalay combines the use of the supernatural spiritual with material tangible elements of magic linguistically, as well as in practice. Therefore, there are adequate reasons for grouping all black magic and witchcraft under the term "sorcery." This concept includes different beliefs and practices. However, each of these parts are equally disastrous to the people, and everything under the broad term of sorcery must be equally condemned by Christians. Whether spirits or poison, the entire list must be seen as a devastating problem.

---

1 Interview with Bishop Ngoi Wakadilo, United Methodist Church, Shaba province, Zaire, May 29, 1979.

2 Webster's New World Dictionary, 2d college ed., S.v. "Animisim."

3 Edwin W. Smith & Dale Andrew Murray, *The Ila-Speaking People of Northern Rhodesia*, 2 vols. (New Hyde Park: University Books, 1968) 2:80.

4 John S. Mbiti, *African Religions and Philosophy* (New York:Praeger Publishers, 1969; Anchor Books, 1970), pp. 10, 113, 257, 258.

5 *The New International Dictionary of New Testament Theology*, 1st English ed., (1976), S.v. "Magic."

6 Interview with Rev. Nshid Sampas, ordained minister of the United Methodist Church, Southern Congo Annual Conference, January 27, 1979.

7 E. E. Evans-Pritchard, *Witchcraft, Oracles, & Magic Among the Azande* (London: Clarendon Press, Oxford, 1976), p. 18.

8 E. Bolaji Idowu, *African Traditional Religion* (Maryknoll: Orbis Books, 1975), p. 191.

9 Evans-Pritchard, *Witchcraft Among the Azande*, p. 176.

10 John Middleton & E. H. Winter, eds., Forward to *Witchcraft & Sorcery in East Africa* (London: Routledge & Kegan Paul, 1963), p. 12.

11 Sampas, January 27, 1979.

12 Ibid. February 8, 1979.

13 Mukalay wa Ngoi, "Sorcery for Killing," English translation of transcript of message given at Mulungwishi Methodist Seminary, Shaba province, Zaire, 1975.

14 Ibid.

15 Ibid.

2

THE REALITY
OF SORCERY

Obviously, the question of the reality of sorcery must be considered. Many witnesses speak of the supernatural events they have seen. However, scientific proof is more difficult to obtain, so others doubt that there is any substance to sorcery at all. Read what two authors have written concerning sorcery and witchcraft.

Seaver in his biography of David Livingstone notes how oppressive he found sorcery to be:

> Descending the Quango valley, he (Livingstone) reflected on the vast potential natural resources of Angola…But he was oppressed by thoughts of the superstitious terrors, the dread of ghosts, the tyranny of witchcraft, the ordeals by poison which caused hundreds of deaths annually.[1]

Then Seaver quotes Livingstone's observation of 1855 on the matter:

> 'How painful is the contrast between this inward gloom and the brightness of the outer world, between the undefined terrors of the spirit and the peace and beauty that pervades the scenes around us…'

(cf. Livingstone, *Missionary Travels, etc.*, p. 231.)[2]

Evans-Pritchard says that the Azande people had no doubts about the source of the light which he saw behind his hut one night. Evans-Pritchard felt certain there could be a rational scientific explanation for this, but the Azande believed it to be the power of witchcraft which moved through the night. A man who lived in the direction in which the light was moving died that night, and this became proof to them that the light was sorcery power. The testimonies of the Azande people and of Evans-Pritchard disagree about the event which occurred that night.

It must be realized that to the animists who are taught from childhood to believe in all forms of sorcery, any scientific explanation, or any witness contrary to this, falls on deaf ears. Whether scientifically real or imagined, their culture affirms sorcery. Whether visible and tangible, or whether invisible and spiritual, the reality of the problem remains. Therefore, it is not necessary to attempt to answer definitively the question of the reality of sorcery power prior to acknowledging this as the single largest problem which these people face. E. H. Winter illustrates this clearly.

A sorcerer dressed for dancing in Katanga

In noting that leopards, which we westerners know to be real, are not the same to us as witches, whose existence cannot be scientifically proven, he points out that to the Amba people of Uganda, however, "both are real and being thought real have real consequences."[3]

In Congo, evidence indicates that sorcery is comprised of acts 10% to 20% of which are accomplished through supernatural power, while 80% to 90% are deceit. However, since the people believe in all 100%, any one part of sorcery is as effective as the other. Starting with the African view of the assumed existence of sorcery, without attempting scientifically to prove or disprove each facet, reveals the pervasiveness of sorcery in the culture. To relate meaningfully to these people requires not so much a scientific mind to prove them wrong, as an understanding heart to comprehend their problem of sorcery.

Dualism and Sorcery in Congo

The ubiquitousness of sorcery becomes more apparent when the concepts of the natural and supernatural are considered from the point of view of the people of southern Congo, as an example.

The Natural Realm

One might wrongly conclude that animism and sorcery represent the complete African world view, and that they have no concept of a natural realm. However, the natural realm does exist for them and includes all the elements and functions of nature. They see all of these and more as a part of God's creation and not as a development by man. As such, these are considered a normal part of life's processes. For example, everyone considers rain an essential natural phenomenon. The food to sustain life depends on it. The Congolese people also consider death as a natural event of life. Thus the world of nature is recognized as a close companion.

The Supernatural Realm

The people of southern Congo, however, do not define the supernatural realm as precisely as the natural world. The supernatural for them includes all the spirits, as well as the powers or forces that influence the natural realm. To illustrate, let us imagine the complete array of supernatural beliefs (as explained earlier in animistic religion) spread out on a flat surface. Here would be found all the spirits, all the deceased relatives, and all the spiritual forces that cause things to happen. Above this flat surface let us imagine all the events in the natural realm. These events would be portrayed on a transparent layer suspended above the lower surface representing the supernatural realm. Between these two layers a space would exist which permits the supernatural forces and spirits, together with the spirits of the deceased, to move about.

These invisible forces, with no system or organization, would then be used to influence the natural events where and when the sorcerers pleased. They could time natural events, such as death or

29

rain; they could place natural events, such as an encounter with a snake at a certain point on a path; and they could also prevent certain other events, such as childbirth or success at a job.

Therefore, the animistic people are trapped, with no possible escape from these forces, because their animistic religion is a closed system. Sorcery feeds on their beliefs and provides a false relief from a world seen as both unexplainable and often hostile.

Across Congo to the northeast, the Azande people also have this dualistic approach to their world. Evans-Pritchard explains:

> Zande belief in witchcraft in no way contradicts empirical knowledge of cause and effect. The world known to the senses is just as real to them as it is to us.... Belief in death from natural causes and belief in death from witchcraft are not mutually exclusive. On the contrary they supplement one another, the one accounting for what the other does not account for.[4]

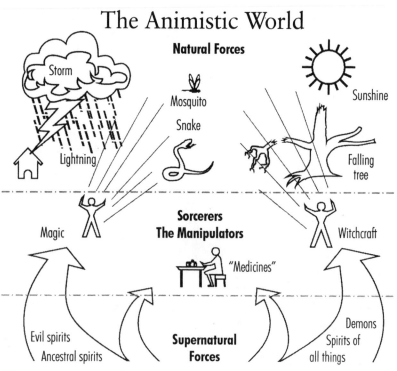

The Animistic World

Natural Forces

Storm

Mosquito

Snake

Sunshine

Lightning

Falling tree

Sorcerers
The Manipulators

Magic

Witchcraft

"Medicines"

Evil spirits
Ancestral spirits

Supernatural
Forces

Demons
Spirits of
all things

Sorcery, then, is neither the natural, nor the supernatural. It is the manipulating of the supernatural forces that affect the circumstances of life. Therefore, it becomes a causative factor behind events. The Azande people just mentioned have an unusually helpful expression that brings the problem into sharp focus. They say, "It is the second spear that kills a man."[5] Sorcery is that second spear, or the "actual" cause of death. Even though a person suffers or dies from scientifically explainable, natural causes, such as a spear or a disease, there will always be a second cause from the spiritual realm behind that natural explanation. This is seen to happen in a chain reaction. That second cause (or perhaps "other cause" is more clear) may be the reason for a single natural event; it may also be the reason for two or more natural events happening simultaneously at just the right time to cause harm to someone.

Sorcery as Related to Illness

In the event of illness or injury, sorcery has strong influence. In such times modified animism and the various forms of sorcery, mingled with immeasurable fear, come to bear forcefully on the victim and his relatives. In the animists' traditional culture all of the available options lead to sorcery. To illustrate, a child is injured in a fall from a bicycle. While recovering from those injuries malaria brings complications that lead to death. The people know that the cuts, bruises, and broken bones resulted from the force of the fall, and that this is a natural result of natural forces at work. The malaria was caused by a parasite in the bloodstream, which comes from infection by a mosquito. When the body suffers illness or injury, weakness may prevent control of the parasite. It attacks the blood cells, causing fever, vomiting, diarrhea or even death. All of these natural developments are easily understood by most animists.

However, when all of the explanations are finally finished there remains that one last question, Who? The relatives are not free to accept these explanations as simple facts, or to dismiss the incident as a tragic accident. They are bound to seek out the cause. For them the natural realm does not operate independently of the supernatural realm. Therefore, some force or some spirit would be considered responsible for the timing or even the sequence of the fall in the first place. Likewise, the malaria followed its natural course because some spirit or power from the

supernatural realm, sent by someone, caused the mosquito to
bite the child at that time.

Sampas explains this more fully, pointing out that for the
Aruund there are two different categories for all illnesses: One is
called the *mayej ma Nzamb*, or a God related illness. These you
(westerners) call natural illnesses. The other is *mayej ma ulaj*, and
they say this cannot be healed with medicines from the hospital.
It is a sorcery caused illness.[6]

Sampas goes on to say that sorcery is not considered to have
more power than the medicine at the hospital, but that it is
believed to be a different power and, thus, the cures are different.
In this, the realm of natural events are distinguished from the realm
of causality up to a point. However, the God-related illness that is
treatable with modern medicines will also be considered the result
of sorcery if the illness persists, or if death results.

Sorcery as Related to Death

When death occurs, sorcery is most serious. As in the case of
injury or illness, the African sees the two realms at work. ". . . basically, all Africans believe that every death is caused by someone.
We say that God does not kill anyone, only sorcery kills. . . . (it follows then) all deaths must be avenged."[7] There may be an obvious reason for some person to employ sorcery to cause the illness
or death. It is just as possible, however, for the victim to be
unaware of any breach in relationships that could result in such an
attack. Therefore, regardless of the insight into the natural causes
involved, there will always be that question, Who? It is recognized
by the victims that sorcery is not a separate entity; it is used by people against other people. So it follows that the question, Why did
this happen? will eventually become, Who made it happen?

The final question, then, that faces the people in any difficult
circumstance is always, Who, then, threw the "second spear?"
While the factors and pressures vary with each death, it must be
remembered that unexpected death is a common occurrence, since
the life expectancy is low. Infant mortality is extremely high.
Therefore, at any given time, people may be bombarded by pressures surrounding several deaths that are very significant to their
families.

The Christian has a special problem at the time of death

32

because his being different attracts suspicion and accusations. Family and friends may not understand of Christians' faith or their refusal to participate in the rituals surrounding a death. At best, they will be accused of indifference, and at worst, they will be accused of neglecting important rituals that are needed to protect the surviving family and appease the deceased. As these accusations mount in death after death, the burden becomes excruciating. Few can stand up against it alone.

Family members, close friends, and fellow residents (friends and enemies alike) are all convinced that there is a guilty party lurking nearby. Traditionally, they do not contemplate an escape from the sorcery system, because no other possibilities are recognized. To strike back at sorcery, they turn to devices within that same system.

---

[1] George Seaver, *David Livingstone: His Life and Letters* (New York: Harper and Brothers Publishers, 1957, p. 231.

[2] Ibid.

[3] Middleton & Winter, *Witchcraft in East Africa*, p. 286.

[4] Evans-Pritchard, *Witchcraft Among the Azande*, p. 25.

[5] Ibid.

[6] Sampas, January 29, 1979.

[7] Ibid.

3

TRADITIONAL SOLUTIONS TO THE SORCERY PROBLEM

Two men who were refugees in Angola in the late 1970's went fishing. That evening when only one of the men returned from the river the villagers became suspicious. Later they found the missing man; he had been murdered with a blow to the head. It was determined among them that the surviving man was a sorcerer and a murderer. After being condemned, his arms and legs were severed with axes and he was buried alive with the man he had murdered.

Traditionally, condemned sorcerers have been killed. While outside influences, especially Christianity, have altered this to some degree, there is always the possibility that an accused sorcerer will be put to death.

Whatever the ultimate fate of the sorcerers, people attempt to protect themselves from the evil effects of the sorcery that invades their lives. When sorcery is suspected by any victim or the family, two things are required—personal safety and revenge.

Seeking Protection

Protection against sorcery power is available at a price. The services of an anti-sorcerer can be purchased if one suspects a victim of being a sorcerer. Sampas descends from a family of anti-sorcerers and states: "This protection will be in the form of "medicine" made from snail shells, horns from animals, from turtles, dry fruit, or even the tumble bugs that roll balls of manure."[1] The spiritual power of the anti-sorcerer is put into one of these various receptacles with the intent to have this power near the client, to counter any sorcery force. This is usually worn on the body at all times. In this sense, such "medicine" is a protective device, and is considered relatively innocent, since it is not aggressive in any way. However, it will be noted that the Aruund in Congo consider anti-sorcery "medicine" to be quite potent, and the art of handling it properly to be difficult indeed. At times anti-sorcerers inadvertently kill themselves. Sampas relates: "If they break one of the rules, or if they attempt to kill an innocent person, then their own magic power can come back and kill them."[2] This is one indication that the power of "good" magic, when used as power against another person, may also be correctly considered sorcery power.

Divining to Identify the Guilty

The first step in either obtaining personal protection or seeking revenge is the identification of the person guilty of sorcery. Lucy Mair in her book on witchcraft makes this same point. She says:

> Since witchcraft is by definition an activity that cannot be detected by everyday means, it must be tracked down by the actions of people or the manipulation of objects believed to have mystical power....[3]

Those who do this sort of thing are diviners or seers who are believed to have that special power or special formula needed to discover who is the one responsible for the sorcery. They may drink "medicine," throw bones that reveal certain secrets by the way they fall, or become possessed by spirits with the powers to give them this insight.

For example, in Congo the Aruund people call this special person a *mwin kupong,* and the power of divination used is called *chiyembok.* This power can locate and identify a sorcerer. The *mwin kupong* is considered to be a friend of the community and is usually looked on with favor, because "good" magic is used. In one sense a *mwin kupong* is considered a protector of the lives of the local people, but in another sense the diviner, too, strikes horror in the people's hearts.

Three tests that these diviners may use to pinpoint the sorcerer involve the poison ordeal. In the first test, a potion is given to the suspected sorcerer. Drinking this will cause either vomiting or death. An innocent suspect is supposed to vomit the potion with no serious effects. The guilty will be unable to vomit, and may die from the poison or become very weak. In this weakened state, hopefully, the potion will cause confession to all that was done to kill the victim and why.

A second method of divination used by the *mwin kupong* is an alternative to giving the suspect the potion personally. In this, the potion is given to a chicken or a goat as the suspect's representative. The reaction of the animal, then, is the indication of the innocence or guilt of the person suspected.

Still a third alternative to these methods is to put poison or "medicine" on a tree or anthill. If the tree withers, or if the ants in the anthill die, then there is a verdict of guilty.[4]

That guilty verdict is a very serious one. The people are afraid of a sorcerer or an accused sorcerer. Sampas notes: "There is an important proverb among the Aruund people which states, 'It is impossible to be friends with a sorcerer.'"[5] As a result, the accused will be quite isolated and the people will search for a way to kill the guilty one.

Conflict may flare up in the village between families and between plotters of vengeance. This may continue for an indefinite time, for people fear the power of the sorcerer and thus cannot always act quickly or openly. In this case, the supposed "good" magic creates much strife with uncertain outcomes. It would no longer be considered simply a protective activity, and would often result in a reverse-curse, where evil is returned for evil. This augments the seriousness of the plight of the people, already restricted because of their fear of sorcery. They must now also fear the results of the only hope they had—"good" magic is suddenly not so good!

The "good" magic may demand the murder of a guilty party, just as in sorcery, but theoretically it would be a justified action by local standards. The only valid conclusion is that "good" and "bad" magic are both evil. Both severely limit and cripple society through abuse, fear, and deceit.

The Sorcery Cycle

Let us consider now the results of the interplay between so called "good" magic and sorcery, which we shall call the "sorcery cycle." Sorcery and "good" magic actually follow each other. With no hope envisioned outside the boundaries of animism, individuals and society are trapped, with power and counter-power mutually perpetuating each other in this "sorcery cycle."

To illustrate, let us consider a common situation. Because of jealousy, a man pays a sorcerer to kill the lover of his wife. This is accomplished with a curse or with poison, or both. Because of fear, relatives of the deceased turn to "good" magic and purchase "medicine" to protect them from any further sorcery. They also turn to "good" magic to discover the identity of the sorcerer and the one who hired him. Actually, a guilty party or an innocent one may be named by the diviner as the guilty culprit. That person, guilty or

The Sorcery Cycle

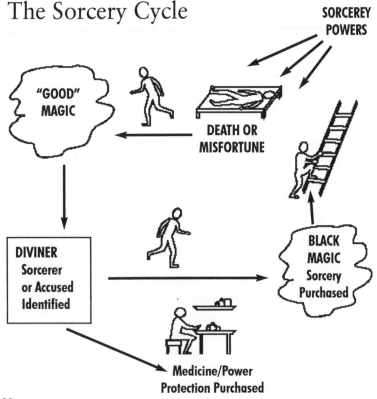

SORCEREY
POWERS

"GOOD"
MAGIC

DEATH OR
MISFORTUNE

BLACK
MAGIC
Sorcery
Purchased

DIVINER
Sorcerer
or Accused
Identified

Medicine/Power
Protection Purchased

innocent, will then be the object of the revenge required by the relatives of the deceased person. To avenge a death, murder will be called for, and this will require sorcery power. Thus the cycle is complete, only to start all over again.

Decisions must always be made with allowances for the uncertainties of the sorcery cycle, even if a family or village suffers. They are not free to decide medically, educationally, socially, financially, or spiritually without taking into account the ever-present shadow of sorcery.

Identifying The Sorcerers

At this point one must ask just who are the sorcerers and whom do the people suspect of such activity? There may be only two or three known sorcerers in a village of fifty to one hundred people. However, several categories of people may be suspected of sorcery.

Rev. Sampas gives us a meaningful list of suspected sorcerers among the Aruund people.

The first category includes disagreeable older persons. Perhaps they have been having problems with their neighbors and have struck their neighbor's children or pets. A disagreeable temperament may result in accusations that end in a curse on someone. Traditionally, even gray hair could indicate the presence of sorcery powers.

A second category is made up of childless couples. Sorcery is believed to be responsible for "closing the womb." If one or the other of the childless couple has children by another partner, then the original partner is suspected of the sorcery that caused the problem. Also, childless couples often resort to sorcery or anti-sorcery "medicine" in order to try to have children.

A third category includes people who become sorcerers after dealing with "good" magic. To illustrate, a person who makes anti-sorcery "medicine" may later become involved in sorcery because of fear. In dealing with the "medicines", one may find oneself in a trap of fear and confusion, and then expand anti-sorcery activities to include malevolent sorcery.

A fourth category involves the children of sorcerers. It is possible for parents who are sorcerers to pass their power on to their children. For example, one of the parents may take the child to a particular tree which has been previously dedicated by them. At the tree a leaf is removed, held over the opening formed by the thumb and index finger of one hand and then popped by the palm of the other hand.

> This is the sign of calling on the certain ancestor who before death had sorcery powers, and the words 'do it again' are repeated in the Uruund language, asking the ancestor to give the child that power of sorcery.[6]

A fifth category includes all people who are physically different in any way. Stature is a factor because a very short or a very tall person is, of course, noticed immediately, as are crippled people and all who are malformed or disfigured in any way. Any such prominence may be regarded as the result of sorcery powers and, therefore, such people may be considered as perpetrators of these powers.

The Attitude of Sorcerers

In light of all this we may ask, Does a sorcerer, an older person for example, react joyfully at being considered a sorcerer by others? In southern Congo this is an awesome position, so such power might be received with much fear. Sampas gives three possible responses of people who are suspected or accused by others. Among the Aruund he says the responses may be:

> a) No, if he has not done anything wrong, and has not actually cursed the victim or planned his illness or death. If he is innocent, he will argue and protest.

> b) Yes, if he has reason to pronounce a curse or to poison the victim. For example, the victim may have started the thing by doing the old person some wrong, thus when accused of actual sorcery, the old person may point out that it was a just retribution and justly deserved.

> c) Yes, the old person may be proud of the potential power and may warn all would-be accusers to watch out or get killed too.[7]

Becoming a Sorcerer

The method by which other people actually become sorcerers should be noted. The actual role of sorcerer is not always sought openly or knowingly. Cultural pressures may force some people into sorcery. For instance, the older people in the first category mentioned above may be told they are a sorcerer by others who have observed their actions. Likewise, children of sorcerers may be instructed to be sorcerers from an early age. Mukalay wa Ngoi, the converted sorcerer, testifies that he did inherit the sorcery power and "medicine" from his deceased father. The family decided he was to be the descendant who would carry on that family tradition. He had no choice in the matter and was introduced to the world of sorcery by a group of diviners while still a child. A hollow carved buffalo containing whitewash and the head of a chicken became the first object of power for him. In this case, the position as diviner/sorcerer, though inherited by right, was given in actuality by older sorcerers.

In other instances, a person may seek to become a sorcerer. This can be accomplished through contacts with sorcerers and usually involves a time of apprenticeship. Once this is begun, new "medicines" and activities will be learned as progress permits. Large sums of money or valuable livestock may be required to purchase such information unless the teacher is a very close friend or relative.

Identifying local sorcerers and participants can open doors for Christian ministry. While it is not necessary to know all the details of sorcery to have an effective ministry to the people it holds captive, it is imperative to know what the people are suffering because of it. Christian ministry to animistic peoples must be Biblically oriented, and spiritually prepared to set people free by the power of the Holy Spirit. No human personality or effort is adequate. "If the Son sets you free, you are free indeed."[8] Conversely, If the Son does not set you free, you are not free!

---

1 Sampas, Ibid., January 29, 1979.

2 Ibid., February 19, 1979.

3 Lucy Mair, *Witchcraft* (New York: McGraw Hill Book Co., 1969), p. 76.

4 Sampas, January 29, 1979.

5 Ibid.

6 Sampas, January 27, 1979.

7 Sampas, January 29, 1979.

8 John 8:36 [NIV]. All Biblical footnotes are taken from the New International Version unless stated otherwise.

4

SORCERY
IN CULTURE

The various aspects of sorcery are all intertwined with each other and yet indistinct. This makes for confusion because no one aspect of sorcery is isolated from another. Each part both depends on and influences the others and thus permeates the whole of society. Evans-Pritchard uses a term that adds perspective to all of the information about sorcery. He speaks of the "web of belief," and explains it like this:

> In this web of belief every strand depends upon every other strand, and a Zande cannot get out of its meshes because this is the only world he knows. The web is not an external structure in which he is enclosed. It is the texture of his thought and he cannot think that his thought is wrong.[1]

Alan Tippett reinforces this concept by noting:

> Animistic religion has been described as the integrator of society. It was not, as alas with the west today, a mere compartment of life, which can be...removed like the appendix from the body.[2]

All forms of safety, of development from childhood to death, along with all the needs of the people, both inner and outer, are tied up with the animistic beliefs which form the setting for sorcery.

Tippett's insight is helpful here, for regardless of the variations of sorcery in different geographical areas, all are part of a total way of life, and thus of a whole system of thought. Thus sorcery is perpetuated by the natural thought patterns of the people. There is no escape from this sorcery cycle for the animist because it all fits together. While sorcery doesn't seem reasonable to most westerners, it is an intricate system of parts which make a complete whole. Mair writes of this cohesiveness: "Though there may be scepticism about the skill of particular diviners, there can be none about divination as such as long as there is no doubt of the existence of witchcraft and sorcery."[3] So it is that one strand of belief affects all the others and depends upon them. Sorcery is not an entity capable of perpetuating itself. On the contrary, it feeds on the sins and troubles in a culture.

Personal Relationships and Sorcery

This web of belief is more closely woven as the relationship to other people becomes more intimate. Geoffrey Parrinder, in his book on traditional African religions, notes: "Witchcraft acts most often upon those who are in close contact with the witches." He later explains that this is not necessarily a family group:

> Witchcraft belief is an expression of social disease.... In the towns men meet many strange forces and strangers from other tribes who may have powerful evil forces at their disposal. To protect himself against misfortune, sickness, unemployment, lack of promotion, failure in examination, and all the ills of life, man has recourse to the diviner and witch-doctor.[4]

Among the Azande tribe it was found that accusations of witchcraft did not necessarily involve the relatives of the victim. There men usually accuse men, and women usually accuse women. Evans-Pritchard explains:

> This is because ill-feeling is more likely to arise between man and man and between woman and woman than between man and woman. A man comes in contact only with his wives and kinswomen and has therefore little opportunity to incur the hatred of other women....

Nevertheless, a man frequently consults the oracles about his own wives, because he is sure to displease them from time to time, and often they hate him.[5]

Regardless of the strength of family or neighborhood bonds, all agree that the basic motivation for perpetuating the sorcery cycle is related to some type of breakdown in human relationships. Bishop Ngoi states:

> If a person is innocent, and has no unsettled relationships, then he has no cause for someone to kill him. If there is no problem, then there is nothing to be done, and there is no effect of sorcery against him. That is to say, if there is no affair between you and another person, then there is no way to kill that person.[6]

The web of belief needed for sorcery is strongest at the points of closest human relationships, and is usually supported by enmity which develops in these relationships. This web, then, is supported by some of the most basic sins of mankind. While many anthropologists would not acknowledge sin as such, any Biblical ministry must accept the Biblical concept of sin to be effective.

Personal Sins Fuel Sorcery

Personal sins that cause strife among people perpetuate sorcery. Each sin may influence other sins and thus be difficult to isolate. However, to understand sorcery at all, we must look at some of these basic problems of human nature.

Greed

Greed is defined as: "Excessive desire for getting or having, especially wealth; desire for more than one needs or deserves."[7] Evans-Pritchard writes about the direct influence this has on sorcery: "...greed may be the starting-point for murder, and men fear to refuse requests for gifts lest the sponger bewitches them...."[8]

This problem of greed is also easily observed in southern Congo. The extended family system seems to facilitate it and encourage it. All of one's cousins are counted as brothers and sisters. Also, all of one's nephews are considered to be sons, and all

45

aunts on the mother's side are considered mothers. While some seniority exists in the extended family, there are numerous opportunities to take advantage of others. For example, relatives often spend a teacher's entire salary by the middle of the month. Farmers who make a rare sale of produce may lose all the cash within the same day to family members who ask for it. Thus greed can destroy all family and friendship ties.

When such relationships are shattered, then hurt individuals turn to sorcery. First, any refusal to give all that is requested affords the greedy party an opportunity to use sorcery against someone. Second, the one who has been requested to give something may also decide to retaliate with sorcery against the greedy one. The first is more probable, since shameless greed may indicate the possession of sorcery powers by the greedy, therefore the others tread softly. Greed may also have a negative side. Anthropologist Bronislaw Malinowski notes: "...such is human nature that a man's desire is as much satisfied by the thwarting of others as by the advancement of himself."[9]

This, of course, would be one of the worst of the various possibilities in sorcery, because it attacks the victim with no hope of gain.

Jealousy

Another sin is jealousy, the state of being "resentfully suspicious of a rival or a rival's influence."[10] In any country this emotion can erupt into violence. In Africa jealousy attaches itself to sorcery. It may or may not be linked with greed. It develops from broken family relationships, from political rivalry, or from any other point of friction. The Azande tribe recognizes this and says: "'Jealousy is not good because of witchcraft, a jealous man may kill someone.'"[11] The sin of jealousy is often the motivation to pursue sorcery. This is noted by most authors who write about sorcery. Either the poison or the spirit power of the sorcerer is needed to carry out the evil plans of hostility generated by jealousy.

In East Africa the same problem exists as in Congo:

> Any man who raises himself to a position of pre-eminence in this egalitarian but competitive society lays himself open to charges of this kind and he must, therefore, be

more careful than less prominent men, so that he does not provide occasion for the mutterings to become serious charges.[12]

Any person, then, who emerges as superior in any way is flirting with disaster at the hands of his jealous rivals. This becomes a serious deterrent to progress. Fellow villagers become jealous if someone else has a better crop, or more wives, or more education, or more money. This has a paralyzing effect on society, because those who excel do so with great fear of sorcery.

Hatred

Hatred is also a vehicle for sorcery, since hatred in turn produces suspicion. As these powers grow within one's heart, they demand some kind of satisfaction. Sorcery is always there to oblige because these sins fuel the fires of sorcery. Whatever the cause behind the greed or jealousy, if unchecked, it sooner or later is revealed in hatred. This may be manifested through an insinuation or some other overt, agressive act against the hated one, who recognizes that "All unkind words and malicious actions and innuendos are stored in the memory for retaliation."[13]

The hated person may do nothing. However, according to Evans-Pritchard: "When he suffers misfortune he will at once believe that it is one of these men who has bewitched him."[14] So it is that where misfortune strikes, personal relationships are broken and suspicions arise. Either party may turn to anti-sorcery to discover the identity of his enemy or for personal protection. Or he may turn to sorcery in order to express his internal feelings in some overt, harmful way.

Sin in any form destroys human relationships and thus perpetuates the need for sorcery practices. Personal causes for ruptured relationships impose sorcery influences on society as well.

Sorcery as it Affects Society

The conquests of sorcery are not limited to individuals or small groups. There are many conquests in society at large. While sorcery involves relationships of various individuals, the entire society is victim when so many are touched. LaFontaine helps us to see the basis for this. He says:

By blaming the witchcraft and malice of others, a man whose ambitions are thwarted and whose efforts are never crowned with success need feel neither guilt nor shame....For although the philosophy which is embodied in witchcraft beliefs declares the responsibility of the individual for the discord in social life, each man or woman can feel that he has been subjected to an unwarranted attack greater than his faults deserve.[15]

This illustrates that society may then point an accusing finger at an individual for some neglect or malice toward others. However, that individual is able to pull up the shield of sorcery to explain away, or at least to ease, personal involvement. This puts an unfair strain on a society that tries to establish law and order with justice in the courts. Sorcery may influence every aspect of a citizen's relationship with society if there is a problem involved. Escape, bribery, retaliation against public officials, and gross lies may all result from sorcery.

Psychological Influences of Sorcery

This is similar to the scapegoat psychology that seeks to slide the blame for one's actions over onto another person or onto some other active force. Malinowski sees witchcraft as "...not primarily founded on the aggressive malice of the sorcerer who wishes to do harm and who blackmails his victims into the belief in it." However, at this point he underestimates the depravity of the human heart, unless, of course, "primarily" allows for many who intend to harm others for personal gain. Continuing he says:

Witchcraft is primarily rooted in the psychological reactions of those suffering from ill health, misfortune, inability to control their destiny and fortunes. As such, it is a translation of destiny and of personal mishap due to the rulings of fate, into terms of manageable human malice.[16]

In a land with endless suffering that is unexplainable, the society is burdened with most of the people shifting blame or explaining incorrectly all sorts of problems via sorcery.

Philosophical Influences of Sorcery

There is a problem, however, in accepting Malinowski's explanation that sorcery is used to deal with fate. Actually, it seems more reasonable to charge sorcery for the vast fatalistic philosophy that clings to African society like a disease. Fatalism is wide spread and is encountered in every corner of society. To illustrate, mechanics may fail to check a vehicle carefully before a long journey because they say: "If it is going to break, it will break anyway. There is nothing I can do about it." A gardener may fail to prepare adequately for the fires of the dry season or the floods of the rainy season "Because there is no physical effort I can make to influence the productivity of the garden." Even more seriously, an ill person may delay too long in seeking medical aid, believing there is nothing that can be done to help because the illness may be caused by the sorcery. Fatalism is the natural result of hopelessly confused possibilities. Surrounded by such endless possibilities, the animist is left with more questions unanswered with sorcery than without it.

More indirectly, the fear of being different, which is fostered by sorcery, is also a cause of attitudes similar to fatalism. This fear may wrongly be regarded as fatalism or apathy. The victims may care, and may believe that their efforts can change a situation. However, fear prevents any such attempt. The hands-up sign with a quick shrug of the shoulders indicates a feeling of "Why try, the powers of sorcery will continue to work out their purposes regardless of my efforts."

Society suffers where such attitudes toward sorcery prevail. Fatalism is difficult to deal with when people need many "willing hopefuls" to overcome disaster. Whether sorcery feeds on fatalism or breeds it is really irrelevant as concerns the end result facing that society.

Current Increase of Sorcery

What is relevant to society now is that sorcery is on the increase across Africa. Some would say that this is due to the availability of more cash to pay the sorcerers and diviners. However, Mair believes the cause may be:

> ...a response to the increase of anxiety among the African population which find themselves disoriented by

the changes that have been thrust upon them, first by colonial rule and mission teaching, and now by their own westernized rulers.[17]

These are factors that force people to seek some escape. With sorcery all around them, it becomes the normal way of coping with otherwise unmanageable problems.

An increase in sorcery in Shaba is also spoken of by Sampas. He indicates that there is much increase when there is trouble of any kind in the land. War, for example, always increases the use of sorcery. Some point to colonial rule as a time of mismanagement of the sorcery problem. However, Sampas indicates otherwise. He says:

> The colonial powers said that they would not judge such matters and they left this to the people, saying, 'This is your affair.' The Belgians allowed the villages to have courts for judging the customs held by the people, and these decided the sorcery cases locally.[18]

This indicates that major changes in society may or may not affect directly the incidence of sorcery. Generally speaking, however, any increase in social pressure leads to a corresponding increase in sorcery.

There is another facet of the increase faced today, which goes beyond the discussion of the usual social factors. Dr. Katenga Mbuya, a Christian medical doctor in Shaba, notes an increase in sorcery in recent times and says:

> ...in these days, many people are returning to the fetishes and to sorcery, because many of the so-called Christians just don't know or understand about the Bible truths. The Bible is now regarded as a book, just like the books about chemistry or history. It is read as something relating to someone else only.... It isn't seen in its true value.[19]

The churches, as a part of society, have failed to teach the Bible as a practical book for Africans. Failure to relate traditional spiritual beliefs to the Scriptures and to everyday life is part of the problem of increasing sorcery today. Tragically, the "so-called Christians" reflect the centuries old problem of a distorted faith mixed with local practices. These failures can tend to increase the fears of the people.

What conquest by sorcery does this generation fear? Sampas surprisingly mentions two old fears. "This generation still fears lightning. Virtually all of the people believe that lightning is sorcery controlled and are very afraid of it." Along with this he listed the age old problem of sexual sins and the sorcery surrounding it known as *dikay*.

> For example, a man can put the 'medicine' inside a woman without her knowledge, so that any other man having intercourse with her will contract the sorcery. It causes abdominal swelling, along with swelling of the testicles, and unless confession is made very soon and anti-sorcery 'medicine' obtained, death can result.[20]

The Scriptures state correctly that "What has been will be again, what has been done will be done again; there is nothing new under the sun."[21] Thus the cycle will be repeated over and over again. Winter describes what faces many animistic people by explaining the plight of the Amba people. He writes:

> At the present time the Amba are powerless to do anything constructive about the problem posed by witchcraft.... They are unable to prevent the damage which is done to group cohesion by witchcraft fears and suspicions despite their awareness of it.... The suggestion that they should discard their ideas concerning witchcraft makes no sense to them.... They are prisoners of their ideas.[22]

They are prisoners of a conquest.

Sitting by the fire one night in front of their hut, Kapemb and his father hear a rustle of wings behind them. When the noise is finished they turn hesitantly to look at the peak of their hut. In the flickering of the tiny fire they can just distinguish the form of a bird. It is not just any kind of bird, it is very special indeed. It is a *yikung* bird, one of the several species that supposedly appear only by the power of sorcery. Its arrival constitutes delivering a message to their hut. Their hearts are gripped by an icy fear as they stare at it. The message is always the same; it is understood by all, "Someone in this house will die soon." Who will it be? Who among us has offended someone and caused them to do this? Why did the bird come, oh, why? Is there any way to find power to stop the sentence of death? Can anti-sorcery help? Could an offended ancestor have sent it? Could a friendly ancestor help us now? Beyond the bird the night is dark, so very dark....

---

1 Evans-Pritchard, *Witchcraft Among the Azande*, p. 109.

2 Alan R. Tippett, *People Movements in Southern Polynesia* (Chicago: Moody Press, 1971), p. 202.

3 Mair, *Witchcraft*, p. 100.

4 Geoffrey Parrinder, *African Traditional Religion* (London: S.P.C.K., 1968), p. 127, 133.

5 Evans-Pritchard, *Witchcraft Among the Azande*, p. 9.

6 Bishop Ngoi, interview.

7 *Webster's New World Dictionary*, S.v. "Greed."

8 Evans-Pritchard, *Witchcraft Among the Azande*, p. 51.

9 Bronislaw Malinowski, *Magic, Science and Religion* (New York: Doubleday & Co., 1954), p. 85.

10 *Webster's New World Dictionary*, S.v. "Jealousy."

11 Evans-Pritchard, *Witchcraft Among the Azande*, p. 51.

12 Jean LaFontaine, "Witchcraft in Bugisu" in *Witchcraft and Sorcery in East Africa*, eds. John Middleton and E. H. Winter (London: Routledge & Kegan Paul, 1963), p. 216.

13 Evans-Pritchard, *Witchcraft Among the Azande*, p. 46.

14 Ibid.

15 LaFontaine, "Witchcraft in Bugisu," p. 216.

16 Bronislaw Malinowski, *The Dynamics of Culture Change* (New Haven: Yale University Press, 1961), p. 96.

17 Mair, *Witchcraft*, p. 82.

18 Sampas, February 19, 1979.

19 Mbuya, Katenga, Congolese medical doctor, Samuteb Memorial Hospital, Kapanga, Shaba Province, Zaire. Interview, November 10, 1979.

20 Sampas, January 27, 1979.

21 Ecclesiastes 1:9.

22 Winter, "The Enemy Within," p. 288.

5

FEAR RELATED
TO SORCERY

A certain chief in Congo shifted his position often as he stood visiting with fellow leaders of his tribe. It was easy to observe the concern on his face as he moved about. Later, it was explained that he was afraid that someone would step on his shadow, and then with sorcery powers destroy him. This man who was afraid of his shadow typifies the pervasive fear which haunts sorcery-bound people.

Sorcery co-exists with fear; in fact, the realities of manifested sorcery are minute compared to the fear it produces. Fear is not always as obvious as sorcery, but it can permeate one's entire being. It does countless damage to individuals and to relationships in a society.

Some people question whether fear is a by-product, or a result, or even a cause of sorcery. While fear is all of these, even so, it must be considered an integral part of sorcery. Fear may exist without sorcery, but sorcery cannot exist without fear. Fear spreads out from sorcery into society, much like the driver ants who leave their colony and spread out by millions to devour all forms of animal life. Fear binds and limits life, devouring all forms of freedom. It is the most potent aspect of sorcery.

It is interesting that two leaders in southern Congo have also expressed separately that broken relationships are the starting point for fear. Bishop Ngoi pointed out that there is no cause to kill an innocent party, and consequently no fear. This was mentioned above to illustrate damaged relationships, but we call attention to it again to note that guilt is often the beginning of fear.

55

Sampas says the same thing in similar words:

> ...if a person fears sorcery with an unusual fear, or with
> excessive fear, then he knows something. Perhaps he knows
> of a relative who does not like him, or someone who has
> a problem with him, or a real offense exists. He knows,
> then, that someone has some reason to use sorcery against
> him. Thus the excessive fear . . . the innocent have no rea-
> son to fear.[1]

Guilt is certainly tied to fear in cases like this. The source of
such guilt is the person himself as he acts and reacts with others.
The potential for fear and anxiety caused by sorcery is augment-
ed with one word used by the Aruund tribe. This word is *kulau*. In
more pleasant circumstances, it means "to fish." However, in a setting with sorcery it means "to fish for the victim." When a sorcerer is seeking to kill a person, all of his actions are part of the
process of fishing for that person. A guilty person can more or less
expect to be fished for. An innocent person is never quite sure
about being fished for. *Kulau* expresses the certainty that sorcery
exists and the nebulousness of its appearance.

There are still other aspects of fear that are tied to sorcery. For
example, an illusive fear is very destructive. Because such fear is
not directly related to known incidents or problems, it may be
more difficult to understand. To illustrate, a particular pastor was
very frightened of the dark. He was a very dedicated man and had
a valid spiritual relationship with the Lord. He was not aware of
any relational problems, but fear was real to him. One night a lay-
man who knew of the pastor's fear took the pastor by the hand and
walked him out into the night. There they discussed the folly of
fear. In the course of their walk, the pastor had a genuine victory
over that fear. It was gone forever. That fear did not result from a
tangible, guilt-causing problem. No, it was the indirect result of his
being a believer of sorcery since childhood. Another pastor who
loved the Lord said: "We learn to be afraid from the time when, as
children, we first hear a cockroach run across the dirt floor at
night, and believe it is a spirit." Every fear is thought to exist
because of sorcery.

Understanding Fear

If this fear is not understood, all attempts to minister will be frustrating and may produce negative results in the work. John Mbiti writes: "Perhaps the most disturbing element in African life is the fear of bad magic, sorcery and witchcraft. These are some of the greatest enemies of society. Every African people shares in that fear."[2] John Beattie writes that among the Nyoro people, a guilty person, or an anti-social person is susceptible to sorcery. He adds this significant statement: "The virtuous are by no means immune, but it is believed that they have a little less to fear."[3] The plight, then, of everyone is desperate. To have a "little less to fear" is no help at all.

Just as broken relationships cause guilt and fear which lead to sorcery, it should also be noted that the reverse is true. The fear of sorcery causes all kinds of suspicion and fear, which can affect every relationship. Barrie Reynolds writes that among the peoples of Barotseland "This fear rises often to the surface and accusations of witchcraft or sorcery are frequently made, for everyone is a potential *muloi* and any unusual occurrence caused perhaps by magic."[4] If people are expecting sorcery to break out anywhere and at any time, then fear and suspicion affect their opinion of their companions, especially if it relates to misfortune. It is commonly felt that "Every misfortune supposes witchcraft, and every enmity suggests its author."[5]

Idowu gives us some suggestions that may help our understanding. He notes:

> The priest, the doctor, or any person of very strong will-power can impose upon the personalities of others psychologically to bless or to curse. The witch with this pervertedly strong will-power always operates psychologically to cause, first psychical, and then physical disasters. The "compulsion neuroses" so much dwelt on by Sigmund Freud will apply aptly here.[6]

While this will not explain the phenomena of fear totally, this sort of power over other individuals causes much anxiety.

One of the most prevelant sources of fear is the power of sorcerers over spirits. In some villages drums can be heard all night until dawn. Their job is to facilitate the traffic in spirits, that is, putting spirits into a person and/or removing them. This is all done for a sizable fee, and often includes an "evaluation." The sorcerer will call up the spirits in a person and ask them what their function is. Then, if the payment is adequate, the "good" or "helpful" spirits will be left in for the client's benefit, while the "harmful" spirits will be cast out. These spirits may also be classed as demons since their function is the same.

Do these evil spirits/demons actually exist, or are they also the fruit of deceit? Only Westerners would ask that question—and because animists believe in these spirits 100%, it is difficult to separate reality from deceit in most instances. Biblically there is every reason to support their reality. Likewise, Christian experience proves their present existence and their susceptibility to ministry in the name of Jesus Christ. However, much of the supposed spirit world is obviously deceit. This will be mentioned again in Chapter 10.

This makes for a certain fear-related behavior in the culture. Children observe this early and soon learn what the symptoms of sorcery are. Marjory Hardyman discusses this concerning the sorcery of Madagascar: "When what is thought to be sorcery, such as the piece of wood, is seen, then the fear which is already present causes the person to show the reaction which the pattern demands."[7] This is a conditioned reflex and may become totally consuming.

Because animistic beliefs underly all of life, the world of the spirits is just as real to these people as the physical world in which they live. Relationships of the past surface in memory and cause fear. Any object may cause fear. Misfortune may trigger fear. Anything not understood or explained may cause fear. Therefore, it must be concluded that fear coats each strand of belief of animistic peoples. It is the unavoidable companion of all their experiences, the haunting shadow of every concept. Whether considering human or spiritual factors, fear imposes itself on everyone.

Granting that all of these points are pertinent and helpful, at the same time it must be pointed out that perfection of performance, as concerns the relationships of life, is an impossibility, humanly speaking. It is not possible to avoid all manner of discord in intimate relationships in terms of natural inner strength alone.

Therefore, while there is in most instances no reason for the innocent to fear, where, pray tell, are the innocent? It is the assumption of this writer that such persons do not naturally exist, because all people are guilty before God and thus are susceptible to fear. Therefore, the possibility of having any victory or triumph over sorcery and its associated fears is impossible within its own closed system.

Sorcery as Related to Christians

The hopeless, closed situation of conquest does not only affect the traditional Africans in their village settings, it splashes over and affects the Christians as well. The Christians are tempted to practice sorcery through fear. Sampas indicated that "Christians may be afraid too, because they have been so thoroughly taught about sorcery." He reveals that many Christians face this vicious problem:

> Doubts and fears come from several things, often the circumstances of life. For example, sickness may come, and bring the fear that it is caused by sorcery. If the illness is long, and if medical help is not successful, the temptation is greatest. Doubts bring fear, and fear can drive them to get into sorcery to counter the effects of the sorcery causing illness, or to buy the services of an anti-sorcery person and thereby get relief.[8]

Sorcery Influences Confession

An important area of the Christian faith which is attacked indirectly through fear of sorcery is confession. Even though confession of sins is an integral part of conversion and of maintaining the Christian life, it is often hampered by the fear of sorcery. It has been observed in many traditional courts that truth is not an easy thing to arrive at among sorcery-bound people. Great pride is taken in the art of testifying in such a way as to draw out an opponent's strategy in the argument. Once a bit of the opponent's tactics are revealed, then only the part of the truth which will counteract and override that argument is shared. It becomes a game, and many are skillful at it. Perhaps a falsehood or a half-truth is put forth, but rarely the whole, simple, unadjusted truth. Why? The answer is more serious than just winning that "game." Revealing the whole truth leaves a person completely disarmed and vulnerable. When their weakness is evident to all, they are exposed to the attacks of any enemy. In this state, they fear that sorcery can be used against them. When most of life is spent diverting and avoiding the evil-intentioned forces that are bent on one's destruction, then to avoid revealing the whole truth becomes part of the instinct for self-preservation.

This carries over into the conduct of Christians who often have a fearful hesitancy to assume the responsibility of bearing witness to someone else's misconduct. Sampas states:

> Christians are afraid to give testimony against another person. If the accused is put out of work because of the Christian, then he will say that the Christian has sorcery power, and he used it through his testimony against him.[9]

Fear has defeated many in this way, because they believe it is possible for that accused person to retaliate with sorcery.

In a Congo pastors' school, pastors were asked what confession meant traditionally. After several hours of involved discussion, one man stood up and said, "Let's face it, it just doesn't happen!" This is an important problem to be faced squarely in ministering to animistic peoples. By the grace of God, confession must be understood, accepted, and practiced.

The vulnerability which Christians feel at this point can only be understood in their entire cultural setting. Since childhood they have always had an understanding that sorcery powers and anti-sorcery powers supposedly cancel each other. When all of the web of belief is intact, then there is some balance of power—at least in theory. From another point of view, it might be asked if a diviner could come into the Church, as an aid against sorcery, and, thereby, affect the balance of power. Sampas strongly rejects this. He replies:

> No, definitely not. The reason is that they are still using magic. ...A *mwin kupong* (diviner) is actually in the same category as sorcerers, and the Church would not accept that person.[10]

This seems to agree completely with what the Bible says against all forms of sorcery (we will note this later in more detail), and points up how impotent all forms of culture are to effectively break the sorcery cycle. Anti-sorcery interacts with sorcery only within the sorcery cycle; it cannot break that cycle since it, too, is a form of the same problem. So, in reality, it offers no help to the Christian, nor to those holding traditional beliefs.

Sorcery Ineffective with Missionaries

It would seem that a missionary who is free from sorcery would be of special assistance here. Unfortunately, animists often place Christian missionaries in a separate category. By this we mean that the animist regards missionaries as people apart from their own culture and problems. Without knowing the missionaries' culture and the problems with which they struggle, it is too easy to regard them as special people without real difficulties. Thus, often the animist does not consider Christian victory as a possibility. Christianity is something which is too often considered unique for the missionary. Faith may then be wrongly regarded as a blessing available only to a special person who does not have to cope with the complexities of the animist's culture. In contrast, one may consider oneself to be very "un-special" and very human. Thus, the Christian faith may be rejected completely, or else there may be a breakdown in his perseverance to follow an initial step of faith.

Sampas brings this into focus when he says: "... the sorcerers themselves say that they can't kill a white man or a missionary because they do not believe in sorcery (ulaj)."[11] Certainly this sets the missionary apart from the daily problem faced by the African. Therefore, Mukalay's testimony has special significance as he relates his eighteen years of sorcery experiences to the Africans. He states: "...if anyone truly believed in God, I found it impossible to enter his home with my sorcery power," and he later adds, "As for those who truly believed (even a small child) when they died, I was absolutely powerless to call them back with sorcery power, or even to see them."[12] This is not the ordinary information which is heard and believed around the village fires, nor is it missionary message material. Yet it is this type of testimony that is believable to animists and can reach them. However, Satan has also blinded many people to the truth of such testimonies.

---

1 Sampas, February 19, 1979.

2 Mbiti, *Introduction to African Religion* (New York: Praeger Publishers, 1975), p. 164.

3 John Beattie, "Sorcery in Bunyoro," in *Witchcraft and Sorcery in East Africa*, eds. John Middleton & E. H. Winter (London: Routledge & Kegan Paul, 1963), p. 53.

4 Barrie Reynolds, *Magic, Divination, and Witchcraft Among the Barotse of Northern Rhodesia* (Berkeley: University of California Press, 1963), p. 161.

5 Evans-Pritchard, *Witchcraft Among the Azande*, p. 53.

6 Idowu, *African Religion*, p. 177.

7 Marjory Hardyman, "The Church & Sorcery in Madagascar," in *African Initiatives in Religion*, ed. David B. Barrett (Nairobi: East African Publishing House, 1971), p. 211.

8 Sampas, January 27, 1979.

9 Ibid., January 29, 1979.

10 Ibid., February 19, 1979.

11 Ibid., February 8, 1979.

12 Mukalay, message.

6

DECEIT
WITHIN SORCERY

In a dark hut one diviner in southern Congo was basing all his answers to clients' questions on the actions of a lizard. The lizard was placed on the table between the client and the *mwin kupong* (diviner). If the lizard moved one way, a certain answer was given. If it moved another direction, a different answer followed; and if the lizard jumped from the table, a very special conclusion was reached. One pastor who investigated this incident found a hole in the ground behind the *mwin kupong*'s chair. A weight which was perched on the edge of the hole could easily be pushed over by his heel when he felt it would be most advantageous. A thin string tied to the hind leg of the lizard jerked the lizard off the table and down into the hole as the weight fell. This deceitful practice was totally unsuspected by the client, who was seeking information that would affect not only the client's life but the lives of many other people.

Deceit plays an important role in sorcery and pervades the whole concept of sorcery. While the poisons do exist, and while curses may result in death, there is an essential system of deception running right through sorcery. The goal of deceit, of course, is to convince someone that what is actually false is true, or vice versa. Three deceitful entities uphold the web of belief in the power of sorcery over the people. They are the deceit of the sorcerers, the deceit of the ancestors, and the deceit of Satan. Without deceit the sorcerer cannot carry out his plans.

A more expensive illustration comes from Northern Rhodesia, which is now called Zambia. A "Luvale man," a genuine fake, convinced a clerk who handled money for the Native Treasury that he could cast a spell over any amount of money and triple the total. The clerk put 500 pounds sterling of the Native Treasury money in a special box. After the proper ritual by the Luvale man, it was to be put under the clerk's bed for three weeks. He was told if it were opened before that time then the money would disappear.

The clerk couldn't wait so he looked into the box. Of course, all the money was gone. He asked about it. The Luvale man told him that he would actually do it all over again if the clerk would get more Treasury money and promise not to open the box for another three weeks. So the desperate clerk put the last 600 pounds of sterling into the box, and the Luvale man performed the spells again. At the conclusion of the story, Basil Davidson adds: "The case against the clerk was heard in the courts not long afterwards."[1] The entire fraud was dependent on the clerk's unswerving belief in sorcery powers and the sorcerer's clever use of deceit.

Not all sorcery deals in such minor deception. Sometimes sorcery becomes a life and death matter. Mukalay explains this:

> I, Mukalay, was a devil. From the time my mother bore me I did nothing else. My work was to eat up (to waste) the money of other people with false 'medicine'. Any diviner or any other person who makes other witchcraft 'medicine' is a deceiver with many lies. He does it to get the money from others for nothing—do not follow them, for they are liars.[2]

It is surprising that this man would give so much information in his testimony which would implicate other sorcerers. He clearly indicates the part that he played in deceiving many people, and notes that his relationship with clients was one based totally on lies. However, he does not say that his relationship to the spiritual power of sorcery was a deceitful thing. When speaking of his false "medicine," one must realize that he refers to the client's belief in whatever Mukalay told him concerning that "medicine," and not in what he believed as a sorcerer. He undoubtedly believed in the powers of sorcery.

Because sorcery is not all it is proclaimed to be, it is, therefore, dependent on the sorcerer being able to deceive his clients. The

Undefined powers of traditional spiritual leaders perpetuates the cycle of fear

supernatural is conveniently slipped into the place of the natural and then anything can be passed off as truth.

A modern use was made of the age-old sorcerer's deceit during one of the civil wars in Congo. Sorcery always increases during wartime, however, this was an exceptional use of deception. Young Africans were recruited into a rebel army that swept southwestward across Congo. At one point these rebels controlled one-fifth of Congo. To insure a vicious army that knew no fear, rebel leaders used sorcery power to inspire their soldiers. This power was believed to protect the soldiers from enemy bullets because it would turn the bullets to water on impact. On August 14, 1964, after proper rituals, the soldiers went toward Luluabourg (now Kananga)with great confidence. Dr. Alexander Reid told of the battle that followed:

> On the morning of August 14, they (the ANC army) ambushed eight truckloads of rebel soldiers two-thirds of the way to Lusambo and practically wiped out the rebels. Any who escaped quickly sent word of their losses back to Lusambo. This turned the tide to victory in our Mongo area and broke the witch-doctor fears and taboos.[3]

Widespread animistic beliefs make such deceptions possible. It is estimated that this army, with its power rooted in sorcery, was responsible for 100,000 deaths before they were finally stopped.

Soldiers and civilians alike lost their power to think clearly and even to defend themselves, because they were trusting completely in deceptive sorcery.

Deceit Involving Ancestors

A second type of deceit may be variously mingled with the deceit of the sorcerers, and at times inseparable from it. Deceased relatives are considered dead physically, but not departed; therefore, they are both feared and trusted. The relationship of the dead with the living is not necessarily a positive hope; in fact, it may even be very negative, as Mair points out: "Hence a sufferer may be guilty of an offense towards men or spirits, or of an offense toward his fellows which has angered the ancestral spirits."[4] This adds another dimension to fear and deceit as the factors which limit the life of animistic peoples, because the people are trusting in a non-existent relationship with their ancestors.

Mbiti has used the most accurate title which describes the feelings of countless Africans concerning their ancestors. He refers to them as the "living dead." These are the deceased from the past four or five generations who have not yet proceeded on to the *Zamani* period where they remain eternally, without contact with the living. He indicates that "...offerings, libation and even divination enable human beings to contact the living dead."[5] He holds that Africans do not worship ancestors, as many outsiders writing about African customs would indicate.

Idowu is probably too kind in his comments about the ancestors, but he goes further than Mbiti concerning the question of worship:

> ...while technically Africans do not put their ancestors, as ancestors, on the same footing with Deity or the divinities, there is no doubt that the ancestors receive veneration that may become so intense as to verge on worship or become worship.[6]

However, he seems to miss the negative impact of these relationships. He does not note that behind many of the supposed contacts with the deceased lies the desperate fear that these ancestors are causing, or will cause, some disaster among the living.

Part of the deceit involved with the ancestors is in the uncertainty of their relationship to the living. There is a common belief in ghosts. Evans-Pritchard notes that there are two kinds of ghosts among the Azande: The "*atoro*, or the ordinary ghosts, are benevolent beings, at least as benevolent as a Zande father of a family." Besides these, there are the *agirisa*, who "...show a venomous hatred of humanity and bedevil travellers in the bush and cause passing states of dislocation." Among other activities, these ghosts are able to spoil the power of poison. "Men say that if a man gathers oracle poison in the Congo and neglects to give part of it to his father as first-fruits the ghosts may corrupt it."[7]

This uncertain relationship with the ancestors is also noted by Parrinder:

> Africans, ...not only fear their dead but also seek their help. Their attitude might best be described in the psychological term "ambivalent," as compounded of both fear and affection.[8]

While he relates many regional variations in the manner of contacting the dead and in dealing with the deceased, the ambivalent aspect is a more generally held belief.

Bishop Ngoi notes:

> Concerning the spirits of the dead—if, for example, a woman dies today, she will not come troubling a stranger. Instead she will be troubling those family members, friends, or anyone with whom she has had some relationship while living.[9]

Here, according to traditional religion, the initiative of contact is seen to be coming from the realm of the dead, while relationships mentioned by Sampas involve initiative for contact with the dead coming from the living. Fear, uncertainty, and apprehension are inevitable. Whatever transpired in the relationships with people while they were living, becomes a gross deceit involving the ancestors.

While some people pray to the deceased and ask favors of them, others fear the "living dead" and buy expensive "medicines" to protect themselves from them. Still others commit murder to be able to use the deceased as spiritual power in sorcery. In any type of relationship with the dead that involves more than reverence and respect, deadly delusion is involved. The results are easily observed and freely reported. Both the hopeful anticipation and the frightening spiritual control are a lie and add immensely to the problems of daily life. No one can have peace, joy, or comfort when at any moment an ancestor may be expected to inject some unpredictable element into one's life.

Mukalay points out that, traditionally, contact with the deceased is very important. This, then, perpetuates the sorcery cycle at many points. John Wesley White comments on this in a non-African setting. He writes: "One of Satan's 'tricks' is to exploit the grief of a bereaved person by sending an evil spirit to impersonate the deceased, purporting to have a message for the bereaved."[10] According to custom, the people of Shaba make the same statement, and these beliefs, with or without manifestations, may leave a Christian facing the family and the influences of the culture alone.

Reincarnation

Belief in reincarnation is only a small step beyond belief in the possibility of contacting the realm of the "living dead." Parrinder writes: "Everything that concerns the family, its health and fertility, is of interest to the ancestors, since they are its elders and will also seek rebirth into the same family."[11] Not all Africans see reincarnation as a choice of the person being reborn. For instance, the Aruund may request that the ancestors send back one of their loved ones. In fact, *Kayakez* is the treasured name given to a male or female baby who has been born after the death of a previous infant in a family. It may be only a partial reincarnation or it may be the same person totally reincarnated.

Traditionally, the Aruund have at least three types of deceased persons who are definitely not sent by the survivors into the realm of the "living dead." These are sent to a realm of eternal suffering from which there is no reincarnation possible. They include: a person who committed suicide; a female who has not given birth; and a sorcerer. Traditionally, these corpses were burned and in a final speech they were told, "Go to the *karung ka misiny*; do not return to trouble us." The *karung ka misiny* is conceived of as a sea of the *misiny* grass. This grass actually grows in swamps and has three razor sharp edges, with tiny serations, that cut and cling to the skin. The evil ones of society must go to this far away spirit realm, wandering endlessly in this painful *misiny* from which there is no return.

The case of the childless woman who dies is in a special category. The reasoning behind the severe judgment for such women has not been properly understood by missionaries until recent years. The problem involves the ancestors of the woman, not her sexual immorality as was once assumed. Traditionally, each family and each generation was considered linked to the past with the children that are born to their women. Therefore, any childless woman had broken contact with the ancestors who were counting on sustenance and contact with the living through her children. Not only was her family angry, but the ancestors were angry too. Both violently condemned her. She could have been returned by her husband to her parents to get a "refund," or she might have suffered ostracism from her relatives as well as those of her husband. She was counted a failure and of no value to anyone. When she died her corpse was impaled on a stick, stood up against an ant hill and burned. Childless women among the Aruund still suffer because of these same beliefs, but the mutilation of the corpse is no longer practiced.

Leadership Positions

The historical leadership positions within the tribe also complicate the role of the ancestors. J. Jeffrey Hoover has studied this at length through research into the oral traditions of the Aruund in Shaba. He speaks about Perpetual Kinship and Positional Succession. Perpetual Kinship refers to present-day chiefs who are holding the same kinship relationships to each other which their eponymous ancestors had many generations ago. This is an external order of relationships. However, in Positional Succession:

> ...a successor literally becomes his deceased predecessor—taking his name, his wife and children, his other social roles, and certain of his property. He is not merely a stepfather or a genitor to raise up children in the name of the

deceased; he is the dead person.[12]

A chief, when he or she ascends to the particular leadership position, must totally adopt a new role. This was witnessed dramatically in 1973 when the paramount chief of the Lunda Empire, the Mwant Yav Muteb Mushid, died. His brother was sought to replace him. The brother was found late one night in lonely agony, wondering if he was willing to lose his total personal identity to become the new Mwant Yav. He could no longer be just the father of his own children; he would be the father of all the Aruund children, ad infinitum.

With no written history to positively date the beginning of these leadership positions, Hoover feels that they probably began well before 1600. The use of these types of leadership appears to have been well established by the mid-seventeenth century. Certainly no dating is necessary to show that this is an integral part of the beliefs and attitudes of the Aruund people and many of the neighboring tribes. Tribal politics are not a separate entity which can be ignored or shrugged off. The people are involved not only with the physical person in a specific position of leadership, but they are supposedly involved at the same time with the tribal ancestors who historically held that position.

Hoover seems to see that the whole thing was a political innovation designed to "…counter the devisive tendencies of individual title holder's increasingly separate families." He later asks: "But where did this useful concept of Perpetual Kinship come from, if not from Positional Succession?"[13] Perhaps it was not, in fact, from Positional Succession or from any other politically related concept at all.

Let us consider another possibility—that of the overwhelming problem of maintaining a satisfactory relationship with the deceased. Since their belief includes the direct involvement of the deceased, for good or for evil, would it not be useful to honor those ancestors or even to control them, by replacing them with a successor who took their identity? The "living dead" would thus be a vital factor in tribal life.

The "living dead" likewise become a vital factor in sorcery, both using it and being used by it. This further limits life for the people, because all of life must relate to the ancestors, even as it relates to the chiefs. The input of fear increases and life becomes more restricted, as chance for error increases. Life cannot be positive, regardless of the jovial expressions which may temporarily indicate otherwise. It becomes a game of avoiding or appeasing one devastating influence after the other, real or illusionary, which threaten everyone on each side.

We may ask at this point, Are these various aspects of sorcery only literary conjecture? Even though one can trace historical factors to the sixteenth century related to this problem, can it be said that somewhere in the heart of Africa lies the source of the problems that face them today? If we could open the closed chapters of history in Africa that extend beyond the reaches of even oral tradition, would we find there the explanation of these cultural phenomena that join forces to become THE big problem for the Church today? There must be at this point an emphatic "no" to these questions. The answer lies beyond local history. The answer is found in the deceit of Satan.

The Deceit of Satan

The first two deceitful relationships considered above (concerning the sorcerers and the ancestors) are anthropologically and culturally oriented. These form the usual categories for studying the sorcery problem. Most discussions of sorcery do not mix Christian theology with anthropology. However, the aspects of sorcery considered up to this point only form a foundation of understanding upon which a Christian ministry is to be established. Therefore, it is necessary to consider the third deceitful content of sorcery in order to put the elements of this foundation in perspective.

Two hypotheses are to be presented at this point concerning Satan's deceitfulness. The first is, that once man has departed from Divine truth, as surely all men have from the fall of Adam, then they are subject to the various forms of deception Satan wishes to present to them. They no longer have any reference point for their religion or their world view. Therefore, all their groping and aspiring is deformed and inadequate. Within a framework which they can perceive and believe, Satan hands a people whatever forms of deception fit their own particular vulnerability.

The second hypothesis is, that any combination of factors relat-

photo by Lena Ellinger

Assorted sorcery "medicines" and idols for sale in Congo

ing to sorcery are just as effective as any other combination. That is to say, one sorcerer may call for the nose and tail of a rat (as in Mukalay's case) in order to manifest the power of sorcery. Another may perform special rituals or make different kinds of "medicines." Such factors may be endlessly different for different situations and different people.

This indicates that the power of sorcery lies in the Deceptor who is behind all sorcery. This power is manifested in deceit, first of the sorcerer by Satan, and then of the sorcerer's clients through him. Therefore, the particular ingredients for any kind of sorcery, and their combinations, are totally irrelevant in themselves. Anything at all is usable, just as long as it perpetuates the fraud and convinces the gullible client to believe explicitly in its power.

Behind the sorcerers stands the great liar, the master of all fraud and deceit, the twister of all truth. People are no match for him, thus, sorcerers are pliable in his hands. Satan molds each one differently, yet makes him similar enough to fellow sorcerers to be believable, both to himself and to others. In turn sorcerers, being deceived, become the deceiver of all who come in contact with them, using and perpetuating local beliefs. Does this, then, rule out the actual spiritual power that is said to be used by sorcerers? Are they only merchants of deceit and nothing else?

Scriptural Evidence of Satan's Deceit

The greatest folly of all would be to consider Satan a powerless liar. He is called by Jesus "the prince of this world."[14] He is not only referred to by Paul as "the prince of the power of the air," but also, very pointedly, as "the spirit who is now at work in those who are disobedient."[15] As he struggles against God and the work of Jesus Christ, Satan is noted as the "god of this world"[16] who is able to blind the minds of people. John also refers to this, saying: ". . . the whole world is under the control of the evil one."[17] Therefore, taking careful note of these Scriptures, let us assume the power of Satan, that it is real, and that it is present in these days. It is seen and used in various ways by sorcerers.

What concerns us most here is the form which that power takes in the world. Jesus referred to this when he spoke with the Jews concerning the identity of their father. Because they were unable to believe in him as the Messiah, he told them plainly:

> You belong to your father, the devil, and you want to carry out your father's desire. He was a murderer from the beginning, not holding to the truth, for there is no truth in him. When he lies he speaks his native language, for he is a liar and the father of lies.[18]

Paul called on the Ephesians to utilize the whole armor of God in order to be able to oppose Satan. It is interesting that in this verse we are told how Satan will use deceit. While one translation says, "the devil's schemes," another says, "the wiles of the devil," and another refers to the "strategies and tricks of Satan."[19] All of these express the same central truth clearly. Satan is out to do all he can in the way of deceiving people's minds and hearts.

Perhaps his power and deceit are brought together most graphically in Paul's second letter to the Corinthians. He says: "...Satan himself masquerades as an angel of light."[20] The deception, then, is dependent upon his power to do whatever is expedient in sealing off minds and isolating souls from the true light of God in Jesus Christ. He must accomplish this in a "dominion of darkness"[21] where he rules and is able to delude people. He rules that dominion as the prince of this world. This includes all peoples since the whole world is in his hands (see 1 John 5:19).

Therefore, throughout history and in this present age as well, people have "exchanged the truth of God for a lie, and worshiped and served created things rather than the Creator—who is forever praised. Amen."[22] When the lie moves in and is accepted, "They will turn their ears away from truth and turn aside to myths."[23] Once turned, they are easily bound, even as the woman whom Jesus healed was "kept bound for eighteen long years."[24] Though her bondage was a type of physical crippling, Satan is seen to be able to deceive and to overpower a human with the spirit world with no problem.

This deceit, which leads to all manner of bondage, is the basic problem for animistic peoples. While in some instances Satan may disguise himself as an angel of light, among these peoples he has completely hidden himself from their perception. He works out his schemes through sorcerers and other kinds of belief involving the spirit world and the ancestors, but he himself does not appear. Sampas relates that among the Aruund "we do not have the idea of one single Evil Spirit being the source of all evil."[25] Likewise, Bishop Ngoi reports that among the Luba people "...there does not seem to be the concept of Satan that we Christians know to exist. That idea of an all-powerful Chief of Evil who disrupts everyone is not known or recognized."[26] His plan succeeded.

It is interesting that Mukalay, who is also one of the Luba people, used the term "devil" above. This undoubtedly came from the Christian teachings which he was given immediately after his conversion. He applied it then to himself and saw what he had been.

Sorcery as Related to Traditional Belief in God

One might logically ask, If, then, sorcery plays such an important role in everyday life, where is the God of the Africans? Is He not able to prevent the conquests? Virtually all central African peoples have traditionally believed in one supreme God over all. That one God has various names. The Aruund in Congo have three names for God which are quite accurate. *Chinawej* is the name for God who is over all and who is just in all dealings. *Sakatang* is literally "Father of creation," or Creator of all things. *Nzamb* is a general term for God who is omnipotent. While these names are Biblically accurate and convey the correct meanings, they do not represent a God who is near the people. He is not available for help in daily living, to help them with the problems of sorcery.

The Absent God

The concept of a departed God, as described in many fables, is found among many African tribes. Some say he left when the sky was punctured by a careless woman pounding flour. Others say he left earth because of the smoke from the fires which men learned to make. Still others see that people failed in some way to please God and, therefore, he left. Mbiti writes: "However the separation occurred, it has brought disadvantageous and tragic consequences to men: man was the main loser."[27] Yes, Africans believe that God exists, but He exists in some remote place. They accept the absence of God and assume they will not hear from Him.

This does not mean that prayers are not offered to God. The Aruund people traditionally pray to God for only certain things. Sampas tells of the Aruund praying: "...for the blessing of bearing children, since it is so essential that all women bear children. Also, men prayed for hunting success, and they asked for health as well." They asked with no idea that they were communing with God. They did not turn to Him for help with their sorcery problems, even though they think barrenness is the result of sorcery. Sampas adds: "They have no hope of *Chinawej* giving them help to combat evil or to deliver them."[28] Bishop Ngoi indicates this belief is similar among the Luba people of north central Shaba, where God is held to be the source of all good. Bishop said: "They did not see all that God was doing, so often they said, 'It is my father or my mother, or my uncle.'"[29] The remote God in this instance was replaced by the more tangible deceased relative.

God belongs to the distant past, but the realm of the "living dead" is closer and they believe the deceased possess a power to help them. Bishop Ngoi continues:

> God was the creator, and the ancestors were independent of him. The ancestors could come to the aid of someone or do something to them....The ancestors were available to the people.[30]

Sampas agrees with that, saying: "They (the Aruund) do have the practice of asking a deceased parent or relative to come and protect them."[31]

Isolation from God

Satan it seems has effectively made many conquests of these people through sorcery and beliefs surrounding the ancestors. Belief in a God who is isolated in the distant past has effectively innoculated the people against any hunger to know him personally. They have no hope of reaching him. We can feel the desperateness of the situation along with Mbiti when he writes:

> It is remarkable that out of these many myths concerning the primeval man and the loss of his original state, there is not a single myth, to my knowledge, which even attempts to suggest a solution or reversal of this great loss.[32]

This is precisely why God has preserved the Scriptures through the ages. They alone reveal to all peoples his great love that sent his Son, our Lord Jesus Christ, to reverse "the great loss"!

---

1 Basil Davidson, *The Africans* (London: Longmans, Green & Co., 1969), p. 285.

2 Mukalay, message.

3 Alexander Reid, *The Roots of Lomomba: Mongo Land* (Hicksville: Exposition Press, 1979), p. 131.

4 Mair, *Witchcraft*, p. 106.

5 Mbiti, *African Religions*, pp. 209, 210, 213.

6 Idowu, *African Religion*, pp. 184, 186.

7 Evans-Pritchard, *Witchcraft Among the Azande*, p. 157.

8 Parrinder, *African Traditional Religion*, p. 59.

9 Bishop Ngoi, interview.

10 John Wesley White, *The Devil* (Wheaton: Tyndale House Publishers, Inc., 1971), p. 40.

11 Parrinder, op. cit., p. 59.

12 J. Jeffrey Hoover, "The Seduction of Ruwej: Reconstructing Ruund History" (Ph.D. dissertation, Yale University, 1978), p. 113.

13 Ibid., pp. 118, 119.

14 John 12:31.

15 Eph. 2:2.

16 2 Cor. 4:4 [RSV].

17 1 John 5:19.

18 John 8:44.

19 Eph. 6:11 [NIV], [KJV], [LB].

20 2 Cor. 11:14.

21 Col. 1:13.

22 Rom. 1:25.

23 2 Tim. 4:4.

24 Luke 13:10-16.

25 Sampas, February 8, 1979.

26 Bishop Ngoi, interview.

27 John S. Mbiti, *African Religions and Philosophies* (New York: Praeger Publishers, 1969; Anchor Books, 1970), p. 126.

28 Sampas, op. cit.

29 Bishop Ngoi, interview·

30 Ibid.

31 Sampas, February 8, 1979.

32 Mbiti, *African Philosophies*, p. 127.

PART II

A SCRIPTURAL MINISTRY
FOR FREEDOM

7

SCRIPTURAL RELEVANCY TO THE SORCERY PROBLEM

Preaching based on the scriptural facts, plus teaching the meaning and pertinence of the Scriptures, are the means of delivering people bound by sorcery. There is no human strength nor human wisdom that can deal with the situation. Spirit filled evangelistic preaching from the Bible, which regards sorcery as a sin, but a forgivable sin, should direct people to a definite time of confession and repentance that will make a definite break with their past beliefs and practices. This is precisely the first work of the Holy Spirit in those who are in bondage.

Next comes the divine gift of salvation which replaces the old with new faith in Jesus Christ. The Holy Spirit comes into the heart of the believer at the moment of faith and begins his work of empowering the believer to stand as a Christian and to withstand the attacks of Satan. New Christians must be taught carefully as outlined here, so their decision is reinforced and so they have God's Word to support them as well as to protect them from error.

There is a logical progression with each section of this chapter building on the previous ones. Beginning with the animist's God as revealed by Scripture, moving on to their God's opinion of sorcery, which includes no favoritism, will help to bring the Holy Spirit's conviction and repentance.

Successful ministry to free sorcery-bound people is very rare. Wherever such a ministry is found, it is always the result of a ministry based on the Scriptures. Over the centuries these Scriptures have proven to be pertinent, practical, and powerful for all cultures, and their validity is still being demonstrated today.

Both the Old and New Testaments explain God's concern for sorcery and what He planned for His people. In Hebrews we read: "In the past God spoke to our forefathers through the prophets at many times and in various ways, but in the last days he has spoken to us by his Son."[1] He has indeed spoken and it is essential to teach His truth in order to have a factual base for a ministry. It is only in God's Word that we find information about a Power that is superior to Satan's.

Education, legislation, scientific evidence, and nominal Christianity have all failed to overcome the impetus of the sorcery problem. All such approaches which did not use the Scriptures as a base for the work of the Living Christ through the power of the Holy Spirit have failed to produce any relief from the problem of sorcery. Mankind, with worldly wisdom, secular education, psychological insights, and materialistic development has never been able to cope with sorcery successfully among the animists.

The Danger of Syncretism

Too often Christianity has not been presented as being interested in the sorcery problem which people face, or if interested, it has not been shown to be adequate and practical for dealing with such matters. A trunkated Christianity is indeed found wanting and vulnerable, resulting in a "neither-nor" mixture of religions. Such mixing is called "syncretism." David Hesselgrave, noted author and missiologist, defines this problem clearly for us:

> When respondents choose parts of the Christian message which appeal to them and, rejecting other parts of the message, incorporate the accepted elements into non-Christian religious systems to make a new whole, the result is syncretism.[2]

People who hear the Christian message may become interested in only certain parts of it and accept only those parts. At the same time certain elements in their own religion are so important to them that they retain them. Relevant to this ministry is the fact that sorcery is usually the part retained from local culture. Mair men-

82

tions this; she says:

> What happens is a rather subtle interpenetration of two systems.... What are tenaciously preserved are the magical elements that give individuals the promise of success, protection and remedies in distress—hence, above all, the belief in witchcraft. Africans and Melanesians do not usually reject Christianity until they have tried it, and then they do not profane it but produce modified versions that accord better with their hopes and values.[3]

The process of syncretism evolves slowly. There may not be a conscious rejection of certain aspects of Christianity, but rather an unconscious neglect of them. Any parts of religion that are irrelevant to the people will be rejected in favor of the old customs that are familiar.

Doutreloux writes about these religious movements in African cultures:

> The different movements contaminate each other and are often inextricably mingled. The people, moreover, pass easily from one prophetism to another, according to the momentary prestige of some prophet or some sect.[4]

While Doutreloux must be faulted for comments in other parts of his study of African cultures, he is correct in his analysis of the syncretistic shifts. In these changes sorcery continues to be an important factor, because the people still face the same struggles and fears as they did prior to the change. Shopping for religious satisfaction makes good sense to spiritually hungry people.

Christianity has been applied to cultures for almost 2,000 years, and where it was accepted without syncretism it was found to be complete and relevant. This ministry, based on the inerrancy of the Scriptures as the sole authority for Christianity, can avoid syncretism as sorcery-bound poeple are set free in the deepest spiritual sense. Likewise, a lesser view of the Scriptures, with an inadequate presentation of this ministry, can open wide the syncretistic doors of assorted mixtures. This must be avoided at all costs, because the syncretistic distortion of Christian truth is more difficult to approach with the Truth than animistic belief.

As we turn now to the development of this ministry, the reader must keep in mind the fact that commentaries and other Scriptural aids are not always available among the people for whom this ministry is developed. Therefore, some of the details may seem elemental to the western mind.

The Bible Reveals the Animist's God

Some people consider the Bible to be a "foreign" book to animistic people. It comes from foreign languages, it has been introduced by foreign missionaries, and when translated it is printed in foreign countries. However, when one observes people reading a dynamic translation in their own language and sees the inner light of understanding reflected on their faces, it must be conceded that it is their book. Animists see their God in the Scriptures, who is the God over all gods. This is the God who is the Power behind all other powers—the absent God of the animist.

The God of the animist is the God of creation found in the first two chapters of Genesis. Local concepts of creation may vary, but the animists recognize that the Creator is behind the existence of all things. Therefore, the omnipotent God is understood by them. Likewise, they comprehend the God of judgment as revealed in the Scriptures. The judgment of Adam and Eve in Genesis 3, the flood sent in condemnation of the evil world in Genesis 6-8, the judgment of Ananias and Sapphira in Acts 5, and the judgment of the animistic people today are generally understood to be the work of God.

At the same time, the God of Scripture has many attributes not perceived by the animists. For instance, they do not know (from their traditional religion) that God is omnipresent. They know God is there, but they do not know that God is here now. Neither do they understand that God loves them, nor that He is a God of grace, mercy, and wisdom. The animists also do not know of the patience of God as He worked with Israel, nor of the love of God when He sent His Son Jesus Christ. These are examples of the incompleteness of the animists concept of God.

It needs to be said that the Scriptures do not introduce a new and different God to the animists. On the contrary, the Scriptures correct and complete their existing concepts of God. The teaching of the Scriptures should begin at this point—where they touch the culture. As the Scriptures identify and reveal the animist' God, the credibility of the Scriptures will increase. Such use of the Bible will assure them that it is not a foreign book.

The Bible Deals with Sorcery

The Scriptures use many terms to deal with the problem of sorcery and its related practices. This complicates the study of the problem; however, it is fortunate that so many facets are covered. No one term or category is sufficient to explain the whole picture, so the broad Scriptural coverage is pertinent. Concerning the different terms or aspects of animistic religion, Tippett points out that one Biblical word, "idolatry" is sufficient to take care of all of them. He writes:

> We could break down the whole animistic system of the biblical world into categories for study, but in the last analysis the Bible disposes of them as a single category in the first two commandments (Exod. 20:2-6)—anything that would usurp the Lord's place in the life of his people and set itself in God's place is grouped together as "over against Him" and idolatrous.[5]

In one sense, then, it is useless to deal with each part, knowing that all are a part of the one problem of rebellious idolatry. While conceding this point, at the same time we must deal with the various facets; otherwise, the animists will not be able to see their own problem (whatever their particular situation) in the Scriptures. Neglecting such details could lead either to their dismissing their particular brand of sorcery as an exception to Scriptural sorcery, or to despairing because their problem has not been treated. The Scriptures are practical as concerns sorcery and must be shown to be comprehensive in treating the sorcery problem.

The validity of the Scriptures for the animist lies in these two areas: the Scriptures speak about the animist's God and they speak about the animist's problems. We will look at Scripture to first see the direct references to sorcery in the Old and New Testaments. Second, we will note the indirect references to sorcery in order to have a comprehensive view. Third, the victory one can learn about in the Scriptures will be considered, so the power of the Living Christ can be revealed by the Holy Spirit. These three divisions need to be taught in this order following the teaching of the attributes of God. It is to be noted that these divisions build progressively toward the goal of the presence of the Holy Spirit, who convicts those who are in sorcery of the sinfulness of such practices in any form. This should lead the sinners to repentance and turns them to God for mercy. Only then should the victory of the gospel of Jesus Christ be offered as the only freedom possible from sorcery.

The Scriptures have much to say concerning sorcery. Many of the references are very precise and thus easily distinguish sorcery from other practices. Other references are not so clearly defined even though they still relate to sorcery. The terminology is mixed and many shades of meaning are involved. While noting these differences, we will need to recall that our earlier definition of sorcery included witchcraft and magic. Realizing both the diversity and the unity of these concepts, we will deal first with the direct references to sorcery and then later with the indirect references.

Direct Scriptural References to Sorcery

God's evaluation is very basic to all the comments about sorcery in the Scriptures. In Numbers, the reluctant prophet, Balaam, spoke God's message to Balak who sought to curse Israel. God says:

> God brought them out of Egypt; they have the strength of a wild ox. There is no sorcery against Jacob, no divination against Israel.[6]

A curse against the children of Israel was useless in the eyes of God because they were His children and He is over all things. God gave a similar message to the prophet Isaiah. God said:

> I am the LORD, who has made all things, who alone stretched out the heavens, who spread out the earth by myself, who foils the signs of false prophets and makes fools of diviners, who overthrows the learning of the wise and turns it into nonsense,[7]

God is also God of the sorcerers and all they attempt to do. In Isaiah we find God mocking the sorceries of Babylon. He tells them of future tragedies and says:

> They will come upon you in full measure, in spite of your many sorceries and all your potent spells....Disaster will come upon you, and you will not know how to conjure it away.[8]

God continues to taunt them about their astrology and their magic, declaring that these will be of no avail against the judgment of God which is coming upon them. Throughout chapter forty-seven in Isaiah the position of the sovereign God who is over all is basic.

When people first rebelled against this sovereign God, they put themselves in God's place. They wanted to control their own destiny and the world, so they set up the first idols. Immediately sorcery became a part of their life as they sought to control the forces around them. The initial deceit by Satan in the Garden of Eden was followed by more and more deceit as it forced the one true God aside. So desperate was the situation, that specific laws against idolatry are found in the Law of Moses. This orientation to the antiquity of sorcery is essential for the animists. They feel that this is uniquely their problem and more fortunate peoples of the earth are not concerned with it. To convey the Scriptural perspective we will consider the laws that prohibit sorcery, instances of sorcery, and the movements against sorcery.

God's Laws Prohibit Sorcery

The first time we encounter any law that refers to the problem of sorcery is in Exodus. It states simply: "Do not allow a sorceress to live."[9] This indicates that sorcery was present at this time in Israel. It is not known when it began, but some suppose that it was learned during Israel's stay in Egypt. What is explicit here is the death penalty. Sorcery is listed with two other capital offenses: sexual relations with animals and sacrifice to any other god. This clearly indicates that sorcery is an abomination to God.

Later we find a more complete law which prohibits more explicitly the practices related to sorcery. In Deuteronomy we read:

Let no one be found among you who sacrifices his son or daughter in the fire, who practices divination or sorcery, interprets omens, engages in witchcraft, or casts spells, or who is a medium or spiritist who consults the dead. Anyone who does these things is detestable to the LORD, and because of these detestable practices the LORD your God will drive out those nations before you. You must be blameless before the LORD your God. The nations you will dispossess listen to those who practice sorcery or divination. But as for you, the LORD your God has not permitted you to do so.[10]

While not all English translations agree as to the order of the practices mentioned here, most agree as to the meaning of the words. These practices need to be defined and explained because they are so inclusive. The terms directly involved with sorcery are:

1. Divination—this involves attempts to explain the unknown or predict the future by occult practices.
2. Sorcery—a general term for magic and witchcraft that seeks to have power over people and to control supernatural events.
3. Interpreting omens—augurs seek to foretell future events by observing things or events which are called omens.
4. Witchcraft—the use of powers that are internally present in a person in order to harm or control other people.
5. Casting spells—the use of words of incantation to overwhelm and control the mental capacities or emotions of another person.
6. Spiritist (or soothsayer)—such a person may cause things to appear, or raise spirits of the deceased by occult powers.
7. Consulter of the dead (necromancer)—talking to the spirits of the dead, or raising up the spirits of the dead for consultation—not a resurrection.

While these terms are different in some detail, they must be seen as facets of the one inclusive problem of sorcery. There is obvious overlapping of the definitions, as if God has carefully overstated the problems relating to Satan's deceptions in order to make an important point very clear. No activity relating in any way to the spiritual powers of the universe is acceptable for God's people.

He expects His people to look to Him and to Him only for life and guidance. It is a life and death matter: death surrounds any hint of sorcery practices and life is found in God alone who is over all powers.

In Leviticus we find other laws against the practice of sorcery. God told Moses to tell the people of Israel: "Do not practice divination or sorcery." Again He said: "Do not turn to mediums or seek out spiritists, for you will be defiled by them. I am the LORD your God."[11] At this point He does not list a penalty for breaking this law; however, this follows in the next chapter: "I will set my face against the person who turns to mediums and spiritists to prostitute himself by following them, and I will cut him off from his people."[12]

In Deut. 18:10-14, we noted that those who practice sorcery in any of the various forms are condemned. In Leviticus we find that those who go to these people and allow themselves to be taken in by these practices are also to be condemned. This is a very significant point for animistic people. Within their culture they find it is prudent to accuse someone or something else as the cause for succumbing to temptation. Because of fatalistic tendencies, the animists shrug off responsibility for their actions. It is easy to blame the drawing power or the cunning of the practitioners of sorcery for their becoming involved in these practices. Therefore, the point must be clearly made that those who "turn" to sorcery will be judged by God along with the sorcerers.

God's Prophets Condemn Sorcery

This same concept is reinforced in other books of the Bible. The prophet Jeremiah relates God's sentence on the false prophets who were telling lies in His name. God says: "They are prophesying to you false visions, divinations, idolatries and the delusions of their own minds." In this case they were doing these forbidden practices in the name of God. His sentence is that "Those same prophets will perish by sword and famine.... I will pour out on them the calamity they deserve."[13] Here again we see the pronouncement of death on all who practice sorcery in any form. Sorcery always opposes God.

Ezekiel, likewise, records that God's wrath is against the prophets God did not call. God accused them, saying: "Their visions are false and their divinations a lie," and He continues to condemn them. He says: "Because of your false words and lying visions, I am against you, declares the sovereign LORD. My hand will be against the prophets who see false visions and utter lying divinations."[14] In this same chapter God condemns the women of Israel who used magic charms and veils to ensnare the people. Speaking against them God says:

> I am against your magic charms with which you ensnare people like birds and I will tear them from your arms; I will set free the people that you ensnare like birds. I will tear off your veils and save my people from your hands....therefore you will no longer see false visions or practice divination.[15]

The use of charms and veils is still another detail of magic which has been declared unlawful in God's Word. This shows the scope of God's concern for even the smallest details of magic. (A similar pronouncement against false prophets of Israel is found in Mic. 3:5-7.)

No Favoritism in God's Condemnation

The inclusive nature of God's wrath against sorcery does not stop with His chosen people. One might expect that God would be more severe in judging His own people than in judging the other nations. However, that is not so. In Deut. 18:12 and 14, we see how the nations of Canaan were driven out of their country (in part at least) because of their sorcery practices. The point is that God condemns these practices, regardless of who does them. As with any sin, sorcery is an abomination to God in any people. This is also illustrated in several of the Old Testament records. Ezekiel received from the Lord the pronouncement of judgment on the Ammonites. God said of them:

> Despite false visions concerning you and lying divinations about you, you will be laid on the necks of the wicked who are to be slain, whose day has come, whose time of punishment has reached its climax.[16]

Bert Harold Hall in his commentary on Ezekiel explains this passage:

> After the capture of Jerusalem Nebuchadnezzar will continue his campaign against Ammon (vv. 28-32), the east Jordan enemies of Israel. His sharp and polished sword will devour them because their prophets have spoken false visions and lies; the fate of Jerusalem shall fall upon them.[17]

The action mentioned in this chapter of Ezekiel is mostly concerned with the judgment against God's chosen people, but it also includes this reference to the Ammonites and the judgment of God against them. God is going to destroy them, because the sorcery which their false prophets have been using has caused the entire nation to become enemies of God and His people.

Another reference to the judgment of other nations because of sorcery is found in Micah. God declares through the prophet: "I will destroy your witchcraft / and you will no longer cast spells." This concerns anyone who practices these things, for He concludes this section by saying: "I will take vengeance in anger and wrath upon the nations that have not obeyed me."[18] Therefore, the condemnation of witchcraft is just as complete for the other nations as for Israel.

Because the animists know they are not Israelites, they could feasibly suppose that the condemnation of sorcery practices by God, the Creator, would not include them. We remember that the animists of Africa believe that their God is an absentee God. He is not close by because he left the Africans when they ruined their relationship with him. The Scriptures, however, clear up any doubts about this matter, for God's wrath is directed against all forms of sorcery and not against a particular people or nation. Likewise, men and women are equally judged, as were Israel and Canaan. Sorcery is always sin no matter where it is found. God clearly prohibits any participation in it.

---

1 Heb. 1:1-2.

2 David J. Hesselgrave, *Communicating Christ Cross-Culturally*, (Grand Rapids: Zondervan Publishing House, 1978), p. 112.

3 Mair, *Witchcraft*, p. 230.

4 M. A. Doutreloux, "Prophetisme et Culture," in *African Systems of Thought*, eds. M. Fortes & G. Dieterlen (London: Oxford University Press, 1965), p. 239.

5 Tippett, "Evangelization," p. 846.

6 Num. 23:22-23.

7 Isa. 44:24-25.

8 Isa. 47:9, 11.

9 Exod. 22:18.

10 Deut. 18:10-14.

11 Lev. 19:26, 31.

12 Lev. 20:6.

13 Jer. 14:14-16.

14 Ezek. 13:6, 8-9.

15 Ezek. 13:20-21, 23.

16 Ezek. 21:29.

17 Bert Harold Hall, "Ezekiel," *The Wesleyan Bible Commentary*, 1975, 3:424.

18 Mic. 5:12, 15.

8

INSTANCES
OF SORCERY
FOUND IN SCRIPTURE

In the Bible many instances are recorded of people who practiced sorcery even though it was forbidden by God. These instances can teach us valuable lessons today. The person bound by sorcery may be surprised to discover that God already knows all about sorcery and just how to deal with it. Many people among the Israelites, from kings to common folk, reaped terrible destruction because of sorcery. Since the Bible does not hide these instances, we should employ them as tools to bring the Holy Spirit's conviction and to lead sorcery-bound people to repentance.

If the bound people are already freed by God's grace through Jesus Christ, then these Biblical revelations can teach much to protect them from further temptations to return to sorcery. Also, they reveal so much about the nature of God. While God is never tolerant of sorcery, his mercy and his call to freedom are clearly revealed.

Sorcery in the Old Testament
First, we find several significant occurrences that involve leaders. Saul, the first king of Israel, was chosen by God, anointed by the prophet Samuel, and reigned for 42 years. During those years Saul had many problems. He was impatient and did not always obey the LORD's command. Finally, he disobeyed the LORD's instructions in the battle against the Amalekites—he did not kill

their king and he permitted loot to be taken. In the end, when Saul was trapped by Samuel, the prophet, Saul admitted that he had sinned. Apparently he never truly repented, for "Samuel mourned for him. And the Lord was grieved that he had made Saul king over Israel."[1]

The Spirit of the LORD had left Saul (see 1 Sam. 16:14 and 18:12), but Saul sought to inquire of the LORD when he became terrified by the Philistine army. Saul tried dreams, the Urim, and the prophets, but he was unable to get any answer from God. Since he was no longer a man of God, he sought a medium.

Several lessons from this incident with the medium (see 1 Samuel 28) need to be pointed out for the animistic people.

1. Saul had at one time known the will of God concerning sorcery and mediums, because he had enforced the laws against such practices. Therefore, he had to deceive the medium. We read: "So Saul disguised himself, putting on other clothes, and at night he and two men went to the woman." The medium was also acting deceptively, because she knew of the laws. She said: "Surely you know what Saul has done. He has cut off mediums and spiritists from the land."[2] The intellectual knowledge of God's laws and their penalty of death was not adequate to keep these two from sinning. Men and women have not changed. They are still powerless to resist the deceitfulness of Satan. Paul wrote in Romans:

> Although they know God's righteous decree that those who do such things deserve death, they not only continue to do these very things but also approve of those who practice them.[3]

2. The spirit of Samuel did appear to the medium and to Saul. Did she call him up from death? Virtually all texts indicate that she saw gods or spirits first before seeing Samuel. Adam Clarke, Bible scholar of 150 years ago, has an interesting alternative to the standard opinion that she did have power to call him.

> The Chaldee (manuscript) has…an angel of the LORD, ascending from the earth. This sight alarmed the woman; it was what she did not expect; in this she could not recognize her familiar (assistant), and she was terrified at the

appearance…. The angelic appearance first mentioned prepared the way for Samuel; and the whole was done so as to show the woman that her art had not prevailed in the present instance, and what was now taking place was wholly independent of her incantations.[4]

It is not easy to conclude what happened that night. There is a possibility that God, with the angels, raised the spirit of Samuel to warn Saul, for only God knows the future correctly.

3. The prophecy he sought from Samuel did Saul no good. It only pronounced his doom the following day. Sorcery is never credited with good results in the Scriptures. Therefore, no one, even an ex-king, should ever expect to use sinful, forbidden sorcery in any form with good results.

4. We note that Samuel was "disturbed" by being called. This indicates that his eternal soul was in a peaceful state, and that he had no desire to be reunited with this present world. This should bring comfort to those who are living in the Lord. Death is not a dreaded state for the saints. Each believer is a saint, a child of the Living God. At the same time, the animists must note that the spirit of Samuel was not interested in changing the affairs of the living—either for good or for evil. Perhaps God in his mercy granted the warning to Saul so that he might repent; but surely Samuel, though thoroughly disgusted with all Saul's actions, had no intentions of interfering with life. The animistic people must see that deceased ancestors (even prophets of the Living God) are not manipulating the lives of the living.

5. Saul's suicide the following day indicates that sorcery was a desperate attempt by an unrepentant man. He didn't heed the warning of his death to repent, and apparently he went to his death an enemy of God. The deceit of Satan continued on to Saul's destruction. No one can expect sorcery to direct them to life. Paul warned the Romans: "What benefit did you reap at that time from the things you are now ashamed of? Those things result in death!"[5]

Another example of sorcery in the Old Testament is the famous Jezebel who was accused of idolatry and witchcraft. Jehu was anointed king of Israel by the prophet Elisha to replace the wicked King Ahab. Scripture tells us that "There was never a man like Ahab, who sold himself to do evil in the eyes of the LORD, urged on by Jezebel his wife."[6]

After Ahab's death, Jehu went to depose Jezebel's sons, and when he was asked by them if he came in peace he answered: "How can there be peace as long as all the idolatry and witchcraft of your mother Jezebel abound?"[7] The sorcery (witchcraft) of Jezebel brought judgment upon her. She was thrown down from her house by her own servants, for we read: "So they threw her down, and some of her blood spattered the wall and the horses as they trampled her underfoot."[8] Her fate was that which was promised in the Word of God for sorcerers. As queen of Israel she knew all of the implications of her idolatrous life. The prophets of the LORD whom she had killed could have pointed her to God, but she put self above all and was not interested in God's truth.

This points once more to the blindness of those who are snared by the deceitfulness of Satan. The power of these Scriptures must serve as a warning for people in these times. Paul speaks of this: "The god of this age has blinded the minds of unbelievers, so that they cannot see the light of the gospel of the glory of Christ who is the image of God."[9]

When this point is presented to animists involved in sorcery they may easily agree with the Scriptures. This agreement, however, is useless if one goes no further. We noted above the case of people blaming a sorcerer's powers for enticing or drawing them into evil practices. They are often ready to concede the basic truths and powers involved in sorcery. However, they are not ready to concede that they are responsible for their own decision to become involved. One of the most difficult factors in the ministry to sorcery comes into focus here. The concept of personal responsibility must be pursued to make these Old Testament references relevant.

As these illustrations are applied in this ministry to the present situation, the goal must be that they will allow the Holy Spirit to speak through the Scriptures with his power. Then he can reveal to these blinded people that they, too, are responsible for their involvement in sorcery, regardless of the power of outside influences.

The Scriptures give us specific examples of this point. Ahaziah was a very evil king of Judah. He followed evil practices and led his people into them as well. Several excuses for his actions can be listed: (1) His father, King Jehoram, was also an evil king, so his influence was strong; (2) his mother was a bad influence as well. In 2 Chronicles 22 we read: "His mother encouraged him in doing wrong." (3) He had his father's bad advisers. In the same chapter we read: "...after his father's death they became his advisers, to his undoing."[10]

Here are three significant factors in the evil acts of King Ahaziah that were influences outside himself, yet Ahaziah was executed. He was guilty because of his father, King Ahab's, evil influence, but he was also guilty because of his own actions, regardless of the influences of others on him. They could not be an excuse for him. God's justice was carried out according to his law. It reads: "Fathers shall not be put to death for their children, nor children put to death for their fathers; each is to die for his own sins."[11] The prophet Isaiah speaks to this by saying: "We all, like sheep, have gone astray, each of us has turned to his own way."[12]

Sorcery Influencing an Entire Nation

The sin of sorcery is tragic as seen through the eyes of God. Death to individuals is severe, but Saul, Jezebel, and others received their just, severe punishment. However, the whole problem takes on new dimensions when the results of sorcery involve an entire nation. This happened to Israel and we read the report in 2 Kings:

> They forsook all the commands of the LORD their God and made for themselves two idols cast in the shape of calves, and an Asherah pole. They bowed down to all the starry hosts, and they worshiped Baal. They sacrificed their sons and daughters in the fire. They practiced divination and sorcery and sold themselves to do evil in the eyes of the LORD, provoking him to anger.[13]

There are two definite progressions indicated here: first, forsaking the command of the Lord and then ending in the practice of sorcery. Between these two acts, idols were established. Whenever God and man are separated man retains his need to worship, therefore, he turns to idolatry and sorcery in order to gain control of all the unseen and unfathomed forces. Fear accompanies these forces and motivates man to perpetuate the sorcery cycle.

A second progression is also indicated here. "They" did not forsake God simultaneously. Someone began, then other individuals turned, and then they turned others of the family or tribe. It is something like dominoes falling in a game, as each one topples the next one. The severity of the death penalty was obviously intended to dissuade them from this disobedience. Even more important, we see that the death penalty was a deterrent to the rapid infection of an entire nation with the same wicked beliefs.

The apparently severe judgment becomes, then, an act of mercy on the part of God to preserve and protect a nation from the fate of one guilty person. The sorcerer would die because of judgment, but the death sentence would protect the others.

As one studies the history of the kings in 2 Chronicles, it becomes evident that the people were in and out of sorcery many times—at least officially. Sometimes a good king led them to reform and sometimes they continued in their evil practices. The point is, that when the people turned to sorcery and its related practices, nation-wide judgment came upon them. Ahaz is listed in 2 Chronicles as an evil king of Judah who was "...following the detestable ways of the nations the LORD had driven out before the Israelites."

Because of his sins and the sins of his people he perpetuated, the Arameans took many of his people prisoner and the king of Israel successfully attacked him. Then we read: "In one day Pekah son of Remaliah killed a hundred and twenty thousand soldiers in Judah—because Judah had forsaken the LORD, the God of their fathers." It also states that Ahaz turned to pagan gods for help: "But they were his downfall and the downfall of all Israel."[14] Sorcery practices, then, destroyed nations and entire armies because they called down God's judgment.

Sorcery-bound people must face the seriousness of their sorcery whether it is practiced by individuals, by tribes, or by the nation. No person involved in sorcery is isolated from others; as the snare enlarges, more people become trapped. The vicious sorcery cycle can accommodate any number but one.

Sorcery in the New Testament
We discover that the problem of sorcery in the New Testament

is the same as in the Old Testament, and it remains just as serious. It is listed among the works of the flesh in Galatians where Paul adds: "I warn you, as I warned you before, that those who do such things shall not inherit the kingdom of God."[15] Sorcerers will be excluded from the New Jerusalem, that Holy City of Christ's eternal presence, along with others who broke God's laws. In Revelation we read: "Outside are the dogs and sorcerers and fornicators and murderers and idolaters, and everyone who loves and practices falsehood."[16]

While those who continue in the works of the flesh are excluded from the very presence of God, the final destination for them is not to be pictured as some countryside habitation outside the New Jerusalem. We recall that the penalty for sorcery was death in the Old Testament, and this is carried through to the final judgment. In Revelation 21 we find this clearly stated:

> But as for the cowardly, the faithless, the polluted, as for the murderers, fornicators, sorcerers, idolaters and all liars, their lot shall be in the lake that burns with fire and sulphur, which is the second death.[17]

The end of Satan will also be in that same lake of fire. Again we read:

> And the devil, who deceived them, was thrown into the lake of burning sulphur, where the beast and the false prophet had been thrown. They will be tormented day and night forever and ever.[18]

This is the final disposition of all who are connected with sorcery. Included is the first great deceiver—Satan himself. Likewise, each participant in sorcery will be there with him in that final judgment. This is the conclusion of all the enticing promises of Satan. He has no lasting kingdom; his power is temporal, and the power he shares with those who follow him is doomed. Sorcery is an act of disobedience any way it is regarded, and it must be seen in its proper perspective. The Scriptures comment on many of the aspects of sorcery. From its early acceptance by people right through to the fiery end, nothing is withheld or concealed. Truly the Scriptures are the only base for any ministry to sorcery.

There are not many instances of sorcery in the New Testament, but they signify to us that the sin continued right on from the Old Testament times to the time of the early church. Paul expected sorcery not only to continue but to grow worse. Writing to Timothy he said: "...evil men and impostors will go from bad to worse, deceiving and being deceived."[19] It is possible that he meant "magicians" where we translate "impostors," but certainly sorcerers are included in the "deceivers."

The early church also faced problems of sorcery. The first to concern us was a sorcerer, named Simon, in a city of Samaria. He amazed the people with his practices and they said of him: "This man is the divine power known as the Great Power."[20] His magic was very impressive, but when Philip came to preach the good news of the kingdom of God, Simon listened. The writer of Acts says in chapter eight: "Simon himself believed and was baptized. And he followed Philip everywhere, astonished by the great signs and miracles he saw."[21] When Peter and John arrived from Jerusalem they laid hands on the believers so they could receive the Holy Spirit. Simon apparently missed the whole point, for he tried to buy that power, saying: "Give me also this ability so that everyone on whom I lay my hands may receive the Holy Spirit."

Peter perceived the character of the man and answered him sharply:

> May your money perish with you, because you thought you could buy the gift of God with money! You have no part or share in this ministry, because your heart is not right before God. Repent of this wickedness and pray to the Lord. Perhaps he will forgive you for having such a thought in your heart. For I see that you are full of bitterness and captive to sin.[22]

Lessons to be Learned

This response of Peter's is extremely important because it is directed to a sorcerer. Some pertinent lessons which can help animists today are:

1. Satan's deceitfulness continues even when the gospel is heard. A sorcerer needs to be made aware of this, for Satan will do

everything possible to promote a false profession of faith. He will try to substitute some personal gain of money, fame, or power in place of faith and repentance.

2. The Holy Spirit is a gift of God and cannot be purchased. That gift is given to the repentant souls who seek God with all their heart. Satan will try to convince a person who is in sorcery that there is a different way to attain the gifts of God. To purchase these gifts goes along with the practice of purchasing sorcery knowledge.

3. Simon missed the starting point which was, and still is, true faith in Jesus Christ as Saviour. His heart was not right before God, for it is through the gospel (the good news) of the kingdom of God that conviction of sin comes. This leads sinful people to repentance and then to grace that gives them the power to believe. This grace is a gift from God.

When Simon faked this encounter with Jesus Christ his concept of who the Holy Spirit is was completely wrong. This illustrates that any ministry to people in sorcery must teach them from the beginning that conviction of sin is necessary for repentance. Otherwise, the plan of salvation does not logically follow and their experience will be warped or totally fraudulent. The illumination of the Holy Spirit working through the Scriptures must be first.

This type of presentation must continue as long as necessary in order to bring the sinner to the conviction of sin. To move on to the promises of the Scriptures for salvation and power prematurely is to take a deadly short-cut that does not lead to life. For minister and seeker alike, this is a time to hear the Psalmist: "I waited patiently for the LORD; he turned to me and heard my cry."[23] Many animists are suffering because of this lack of waiting, this time that is needed to discover the relationship between God, sin, and sinner. Let Simon teach us an important lesson!

4. Peter prescribed repentance and prayer. This is the answer to any sin or any mistake. Forgiveness is up to the Lord. It cannot be demanded or conjured up. It cannot be received via anyone else. Even Peter could not forgive Simon. The problem was in Simon's heart. Jesus spoke to this saying: "For out of the heart come evil thoughts, murder, adultery, sexual immorality, theft, false testimony, slander. These are what make a man 'unclean;'..."[24] Only repentance and prayer can lead to salvation from any sin.

5. Simon was captive to sin. We have referred to the "sorcery-

bound" people for this reason. Satan has not stood aside and hint-
ed at sin and left them free to do as they wish. Once they succumb
to temptation and willfully enter into sorcery, whether deceived or
not, they are bound by Satan. They become his captives and heed
him. They are no longer free to choose to leave sorcery, to be free
from the fear of it, or to ignore it. They are compelled to stay in
that sorcery cycle. Paul declares to the Galatians: "Formerly when
you did not know God, you were slaves to those who by nature
are not gods."[25] Jesus also explained it clearly: "I tell you the truth,
everyone who sins is a slave to sin."[26]

6. We do not know what happened to Simon. He replied to
Peter: "Pray to the Lord for me so that nothing you have said may
happen to me."[27] He did not repent in this account, but at least he
asked for prayer from a saint. That was a good beginning. Any person who is bound by sorcery should seek out a victorious Christian
who is full of the Holy Spirit, so that they can pray and search the
Scriptures together. They must never think that without God's
grace one can attain salvation and victory, but the help of a godly
Christian should not be overlooked as a part of the ministry to a
person in the bondage of sorcery. James reminds us: "The prayer
of a righteous man is powerful and effective."[28]

Another similar encounter with a sorcerer occurred in the city
of Paphos. Paul and Barnabas were on a preaching tour which took
them from city to city across the whole island of Cyprus. A man
named Sergius Paulus, the proconsul in Paphos, wanted to hear the
word of God. He sent for Paul and Barnabas to come, but an attend-
ant of the proconsul named Elymas tried to prevent the meeting
with them, because Elymas was a sorcerer and was much opposed
to the missionaries, Paul and Barnabas. However, Paul (like Peter
with Simon) had the power to discern the situation and we read:

> ...Paul, filled with the Holy Spirit looked straight at
> Elymas and said, "You are a child of the devil and an enemy
> of everything that is right! You are full of all kinds of deceit
> and trickery. Will you never stop perverting the right ways
> of the Lord? Now the hand of the Lord is against you. You
> are going to be blind, and for a time you will be unable to
> see the light of the sun."[29]

Again we see several special lessons for this ministry to the sorcery-bound people in this passage:

1. The sorcerer is a child of the devil. As mentioned above, Satan has the power to bind those in sorcery, after which they obey him as his children. They learn of him as if he were their earthly father. Sorcery today is no different—it must be revealed for what it really is, with no compromise.

2. Those practicing sorcery are automatically enemies of all that is right. They pervert the right ways of the Lord. This completely eliminates any question as to whether a child of God can be involved in sorcery, or if sorcery can be in the church. These two positions are exactly opposed to each other—they cannot exist together in an individual or in a church. Churches among the animists need to take careful note of this. Without constant vigilance by the Christians, the devil and his perversions enter the church. Certainly God cannot co-exist with Satan.

3. The devil and sorcery depend on deceit and trickery. Truth and fact have no place in them. No Christian can look to them for insight or knowledge or protection. Everything in sorcery is deceitful and corrupt, so Christians must at all costs separate themselves from sorcerers. Paul, referring to Isaiah and Ezekiel says: "Therefore come out from them / and be separate / says the Lord. / Touch no unclean thing, / and I will receive you."[30]

4. The hand of the Lord is against all sorcery. This we have seen previously and it is good to realize the Holy Spirit confirms this stand through Paul. No greater danger can face a person, or a tribe, or a nation, than to have the hand of the Lord against them.

Elymas was struck blind immediately—probably to permit the proconsul to believe. What happened to Elymas after this is as much a mystery as is the case of Simon. However, the basic truths of Scripture all apply to both of them.

These direct references to sorcery in the Scriptures are especially helpful for bringing out the great truths which the animistic people must consider. Other incidents will be discussed under different headings, so we will turn now to some important indirect references to sorcery in the Scriptures that will have much influence on this ministry.

---

[1] 1 Sam. 15:35.

2 1 Sam. 28:8-9.

3 Rom. 1:32.

4 Adam Clarke, "1 Samuel," *Clarke's Commentary*, Abingdon reprint, 2:297.

5 Rom. 6:21.

6 1 Kgs 21:25.

7 2 Kgs. 9:22.

8 2 Kgs. 9:33.

9 2 Cor. 4:4.

10 2 Chr. 22:3-4.

11 Deut. 24:16.

12 Isa. 53:6.

13 2 Kgs. 17:16-17.

14 2 Chr. 28:3, 6, 23.

15 Gal. 5:19-21 [RSV].

16 Rev. 22:15 [RSV].

17 Rev. 21:8 [RSV].

18 Rev. 20:10.

19 2 Tim. 3:13.

20 Acts 8:10.

21 Acts 8:13.

22 Acts 8:19, 20-23.

23 Ps. 40:1.

24 Matt. 15:19-20.

25 Gal. 4:8.

26 John 8:34.

27 Acts 8:24.

28 Jas. 5:16.

29 Acts 13:9-11.

30 2 Cor. 6:17.

9

INDIRECT SCRIPTURAL REFERENCES TO SORCERY

There are beliefs in animism that may not be specifically classified under sorcery, and yet they influence sorcery beliefs. As such they will hinder any attempt which is made to bring freedom to the sorcery-bound people. Without attempting to deal exhaustively with all the Scriptural references, three connections must be highlighted. They are idolatry, revenge, and necromancy. Two special problems will also be discussed concerning the transfiguration and reincarnation.

Idolatry as Related to Sorcery

Idolatry is defined clearly in the first two commandments of God. In Exodus God commanded:

> You shall have no other gods before me. You shall not make for yourself an idol in the form of anything in heaven above or on the earth beneath or in the waters below. You shall not bow down to them or worship them; for I, the LORD your God, am a jealous God,...[1]

This leaves no doubt as to the rightful place of God in the eyes of his people. He specifically outlaws idols. The problem of all sin, and sorcery in particular, is that once God has been replaced by an idol, then attempts to contact spirits and control the idol accelerate. The deceit of Satan causes the sorcery-bound person to press on under the delusion that there is yet something more to be gained.

Idols as such are never given any real existence in the Scriptures. They are referred to as: "lifeless forms,"[2] "detestable images,"[3] and "vile images."[4] Paul says: "An idol is nothing at all in the world."[5] The image as such is powerless and only a work of hands. The Psalmist gives the most complete description:

> But their idols are silver and gold,
>   made by the hands of men.
> They have mouths, but cannot speak,
>   eyes, but they cannot see;
> they have ears, but cannot hear,
>   noses, but they cannot smell;
> they have hands, but cannot feel,
>   feet, but they cannot walk;
> nor can they utter a sound with
>   their throats.[6]

photo by William R. Harvey

Idols such as this one are an open door to Sorcery and the bondage that it brings.

So where lies the danger? The Scriptures point out that behind the idols there exists the world of demons and spirits. These idols are what intercept man's attention and turn him to themselves. The danger lies beyond, or behind the idol. The Old Testament indicates this as we read:

> They made him (God) jealous with their
>   foreign gods
> and angered him with their
>   detestable idols.
> They sacrificed to demons, which are
>   not God—
> gods they had not known,
> gods that recently appeared,
> gods your fathers did not fear.[7]

The New Testament takes this same position when Paul writes:

> Do I mean then that a sacrifice offered to an idol is anything, or that an idol is anything? No, but the sacrifices of pagans are offered to demons, not to God, and I do not want you to be participants with demons. You cannot drink the cup of the Lord and the cup of demons, too; you cannot have a part in both the Lord's table and the table of demons.[8]

It is, therefore, on these grounds that idolatry must be most severely condemned. Not only is it a rejection of the one true God; it is also a turning to demons and to devils—to Satan himself. It is at this point that idolatry and sorcery meet and mingle. In the various lists of sins in Gal. 5:19, Eph. 5:5, Col. 3:5, Rev. 9:20; 21:8; 22:15, sorcery and idolatry are both listed. When a person turns from God, of course, there is no limit to the extent of one's sins, since each one adds to the other.

The animist's situation is very closely related to that which is explained in the Scriptures. Idolatry and sorcery are found together. They are not separate entities, but are part of the same program that continuously and progressively leads the people away from God. Those who are idolaters need not think that they can turn

God. Those who are idolaters need not think that they can turn from idols without turning from sorcery; neither can those in sorcery turn from their practices without also turning from idolatry. They are interrelated.

Turning from idols became a Christian credential for the Thessalonians. Paul recognized the genuineness of their repentance because of the testimony of others and said of them: "They tell how you turned to God from idols to serve the living and true God, ..."[9] Turning from the idols was part of the turning to God. They go together. This is expressed in a negative way in Revelation where we read:

> The rest of mankind who were not killed by these plagues still did not repent of the work of their hands; they did not stop worshiping demons, and idols of gold, silver, bronze, stone and wood—idols that cannot see or hear or walk. Nor did they repent of their murders, their magic arts, their sexual immorality or their thefts.[10]

For these people there was no repentance because they could not give up the idols nor cease from their sorcery and other sins. How utterly important it is for the animists to realize that idolatry and sorcery are a part of the entire system of revolt against God. Any facet of these beliefs and practices will remain as a barrier between them and God if such sins are not surrendered and confessed. To repeat, the ability to repent is a gift of God. Jesus tells us: "No one can come to me unless the Father who sent me draws him...."[11] As his Word speaks through the Holy Spirit to the hearts of the animistic people, they must invite his searching and his revelation to reveal their lost condition. Every belief and every practice needs to be brought to the Word of God and examined in the light of the Holy Spirit. That is the first step to freedom.

Revenge as Related to Sorcery

Revenge is retaliation against a person who has wronged someone. This was explained as a part of the sorcery cycle. In the law which God gave to Moses, revenge was permitted for first degree murder; the next of kin was permitted to kill the offender. In order to protect innocent people and those who had killed someone unintentionally, six towns or cities were set aside as places of refuge where an accused person could go for safety until a fair trial was held. The details are enumerated in Num. 35:6-34. One condition that is very important here is: "'Anyone who kills a person is to be put to death as a murderer only on the testimony of witnesses. But no one is to be put to death on the testimony of only one witness.'"[12] God does not intend for people to practice injustice; instead he has an ordered and just arrangement for the protection of all involved. There is no divination allowed; there is no room for magic or soothsaying; there is no place for charms or ordeals by poison; nor is any form of secret revenge allowed. It must be clearly noted that the revenge connected with sorcery, which continually disrupts society by breeding evil, is not the revenge described by God's law. God's type of revenge is designed with only the good of mankind and society in mind. Justice and sorcery have nothing in common.

Many reasons not as serious as murder create in persons a desire for revenge; but whatever these may be, God has ordered that such desire be set aside. In Leviticus one finds many laws that are helpful in human relationships. One of these says: "Do not seek revenge or bear a grudge against one of your people, but love your neighbor as yourself..."[13] However natural it is for fallen mankind to feel the need for revenge and to hold a grudge against another person, it is not acceptable to God. He has established, since the time of Moses, that love is the only satisfactory way for people to share life in society. Without love society breaks down and people destroy one another. Surely God's plan is best. Each animist who has any contact with sorcery faces the problem of revenge. Since each death is caused by someone's "second spear," revenge becomes an integral part of all society. Sorcery feeds on this revenge and Satan uses deceit to make people believe that revenge is helpful.

Jesus said: "You have heard that it was said, 'Love your neighbor and hate your enemies.' But I tell you: Love your enemies and pray for those who persecute you."[14] The neighbor, or friend, referred to here was commonly considered to be a fellow Jew by the Jews. They held that the law to love did not apply outside the Jewish people. Jesus made quite an addition here when he included the enemies of God's people. It seems that he has done this for the sake of the enemies. The love may give the enemies a new vision of what God is like, and perhaps lead them to repentance. Certainly the love shown toward them by their enemies will be a blessing.

However, there is a larger reason for love to replace hate and revenge. Those who hate destroy themselves and cannot be what God intended them to be. The one who avenges is in a dangerous position before God. Clarke, in his commentary, speaks about revenge:

> Having the mind averse from contentions and preferring peace and concord to temporal advantages, is most solemnly recommended to all Christians. We are great gainers when we lose only our money, or other property, and risk not the loss of our souls, by losing the love of God and man....for he that avenges himself must lose the mind of Christ and thus suffer injury ten thousand times greater than he can ever receive from man. Revenge at such an expense is dear indeed.[15]

This is great wisdom, and from it we see that God actually intended the good of his own children when he forbade them to take revenge.

This same theme applies to the commands of Jesus earlier in Matt. 5:38-42. In that passage he refers to the Exodus code of conduct which said:

> But if there is serious injury, you are to take life for life, eye for eye, tooth for tooth, hand for hand, foot for foot, burn for burn, wound for wound, bruise for bruise.[16]

This can be misinterpreted to give full license for revenge as anyone sees fit. Since this is not in keeping with the spirit of the law or with the intent of God to have justice shown among the people, we must seek another concept. Clarke makes a very helpful observation on this. Referring to these verses in Matthew he notes:

> Nothing, however, of this kind was left to private revenge; the magistrate awarded the punishment when the

fact was proved, otherwise the lex talionis (law of like for like) would have utterly destroyed the peace of society and have sown the seeds of hatred, revenge, and all uncharitableness.[17]

Concerning all of the passages that relate to this concept, Jesus saw that the best way to insure acceptable attitudes and actions in a person who had been offended was to substitute love for all the natural feelings that the person had. At the same time, love was the best way to insure the greatest possible opportunity for helping the offender. This is threaded completely throughout the New Testament—love in order to fulfill the law.

It may be asked, then, How can this be justice? God reminds his people that he is a sovereign God—it is he who will avenge all that needs avenging. Paul states: "Do not take revenge, my friends, but leave room for God's wrath, for it is written: 'It is mine to avenge; I will repay,' says the Lord."[18] He refers here to Deut. 32:35, so the concept is certainly not a new one. To "leave room for God's wrath" calls upon the believer to give freedom to God in allowing him to do as he sees fit, whenever he sees fit. God is good—in him is no darkness. He is omniscient and omnipotent and just. Jesus himself declared: "The Son of Man is going to come in his Father's glory with his angels, and then he will reward each person according to what he has done."[19] Therefore, it should not be difficult to trust him with the final accounting of each person and each act. However, this is impossible, humanly speaking, for the person trapped in sorcery, and this fact must be presented to the sorcery-bound people to show the distance that sin places between man's way and God's way.

Necromancy as Related to Sorcery

The third indirect reference to sorcery which we will consider here is that of the deceased or the ancestors. Oosthuizen makes a powerful statement about the problem of the ancestors:

> The greatest obstacle to true conversion lies in the conviction that the discarding of the traditional customs will lead to destruction because they are then cut off from the source which gives them vital energy, life force, to live

strongly.[20]

Traditionally, to be cut off from the ancestors is a very frightening thing to animists. With belief in the active participation of the deceased in the lives of the living, the loss of contact or the ignoring of the deceased could bring great trouble. The use of sorcery to manipulate the spirits of the dead complicates this ministry. The problem of the concept of the dead must be considered or it will become a stumbling block to genuine repentance.

Laying aside the religions of man, let us turn to the Scriptures to grasp God's teaching about the dead. In his teaching we find a definite separation of the deceased and the living. We find this in two statements of prohibition of the use of mediums. In Leviticus we read: "I will set my face against the person who turns to mediums and spiritists to prostitute himself by following them, and I will cut him off from his people...."[21] Again in Deuteronomy we read that there is to be found no one "...who is a medium or spiritist or who consults the dead. Anyone who does these things is detestable to the LORD...."[22] A person who attempted to contact the dead would in turn lose his own life. We noted this in the consideration of King Saul above in connection with sorcery. Saul lost his life because he turned from God—turning toward the medium was the desperate act of a trapped man. It is clear that God will not tolerate such actions.

We look still further and see that the Psalmist asks: "Is your love declared in the grave and your faithfulness in Destruction?"[23] The blessings of God's love for us in this life are not known to those who are already dead. What happens here on earth is not related to those who have gone ahead. However, all of the Old Testament writers were limited in their concept of death. For them, Sheol was a nebulous place where the souls of those who had died resided. They had the hope of a Messiah, but they could not conceive of the complete revelation of eternity which Jesus Christ would bring.

Subsequently, we find in the New Testament some teachings about death, but mostly these Scriptures speak about life. Perhaps this is the basic difference in the attitude of the animists to the problem of death. They are preoccupied with death and the deceased ancestors, while the New Testament is preoccupied with life abundant here on earth and eternal life in Jesus Christ. There must be a turning from hope in the deceased to a hope in the resurrected Christ that guarantees each Christian's resurrection to eternal life. Paul explains this preoccupation of the sinful mind, saying: "Those who live according to the sinful nature have their minds set on what that nature desires....The mind of sinful man is death..." This is the condition of the sorcery-bound people. They must understand that this is the plight of all people everywhere without Christ. For them, the ancestors are a special part of that concern with death. Regardless of how special and peculiar this belief is to the animist, it must be converted too. Paul does not agree to leave the mind set on death. He contrasts it with: "The mind controlled by the Spirit is life and peace."[24]

H. Orton Wiley in his theological work lists the ways death is described in the Scriptures. He writes:

> ...physical death is mentioned as being <u>gathered unto thy people</u> (Deut. 32:50); <u>a going the way of all the earth</u> (Joshua 23:14); <u>a being gathered unto the fathers</u> (Judges 2:10); a return to the dust <u>to the earth as it was,</u> and the Spirit returning unto God who gave it (Eccl. 12:7); a giving up, or a yielding of the ghost (Acts. 5:5, 10); a dissolving of <u>our earthly house of this tabernacle</u> (2 Cor. 5:1); and a being <u>absent from the body and present with the Lord</u> (2 Cor. 5:8).[25]

The Scriptures teach us that there is an intermediate state between life on this earth and the eternal abode of the soul. The righteous (in Christ Jesus) will enter their final eternal state only at the final judgment by Jesus Christ. This judgment is explained in detail in Matt. 25:31-46. Until that time comes, the Scriptures indicate the righteous will go to be immediately with Christ and God. No delay or period of waiting to enter this intermediate state is ever mentioned. Paul declares: "We are confident, I say, and would prefer to be away from the body and at home with the Lord."[26] There is no mention of being away to wait in some place until the resurrection of the dead. Jesus told the repentant criminal crucified with him: "I tell you the truth, today you will be with me in paradise."[27] Therefore, those who die in sin are believed to go immediately to a place apart from the Lord, for no sin can exist in the presence of God. Futhermore, for both the righteous and the sinner, their souls are conscious during that time. They are not unconscious or in a state of limbo. In Romans we read:

> For I am convinced that neither death nor life, neither angels nor demons, neither the present nor the future, nor any powers, neither height nor depth, nor anything else in all creation, will be able to separate us from the love of God that is in Christ Jesus our Lord.[28]

This presence with God is continuous for those who are genuinely his, and according to the Revelation of Jesus Christ, at the time of death those who are in the Lord enter a time of rest where they are blessed in his presence. We read: "...Blessed are the dead who die in the Lord from now on. 'Yes,' says the Spirit, 'they will rest from their labor, for their deeds will follow them.'"[29] The sinners, of course, are denied the rest and are in a place of suffering and unrest.

This is the basic teaching of the Scriptures concerning death and the state of the soul after death. It must be noted that there is no provision for contact back and forth between the realm of the dead and the living as found in Luke 16:19-31. Nothing important is omitted from the Scriptures. Jesus Christ said: "...I have called you friends, for everything that I learned from my Father I have made known to you."[30] And Peter tells us: "His divine power has given us everything we need for life and godliness through our knowledge of him who called us."[31] God's Word is a true and sufficient guide to faith and eternal life. The silence is significant, because anything as important as this (according to the animists) would surely have been expounded upon thoroughly. Therefore, one must reach the conclusion that contact with the ancestors, ancestor worship, and the fear surrounding these must be of the devil and not of God. It is strictly forbidden in the Scriptures, but not denied as a possibility. That is to say, it may be very real, but it is not of God and, therefore, it cannot be a part of a Christian's life.

Ancestors and Reincarnation

The animists link another problem to that of the ancestors. It is the question of reincarnation. The new birth, or second birth, might pose problems for some people. The Bible tells us that Nicodemus was troubled by it. John relates: "How can a man be born when he is old?" Nicodemus asked: "Surely he cannot enter a second time into his mother's womb to be born!" Jesus answered this very clearly, stating that there needs to be two births. We read:

> Jesus answered, 'I tell you the truth, unless a man is born of water and the Spirit, he cannot enter the kingdom of God. Flesh gives birth to flesh, but the Spirit gives birth to spirit....[32]

It is the mother who gives birth to a child—first birth. It is the Holy Spirit who gives spiritual life to a believer—second birth. That second birth is into the kingdom of God and from there one does not enter and leave.

One life is indicated in the Scriptures for each soul created. We read: "...man is destined to die once, and after that to face judgment,..."[33] The one life is lived in such a way that it will be acceptable to God (through faith in Jesus Christ) or it will be condemned by its own actions by a just God. The judgment will come once for all people of all time. There is no provision or any possibility for reincarnation to take place in the order of creation.

The animists must be shown that the same characteristics that produced a child in one form at one time will also be at work when another is born. Therefore, it is quite possible for a child to resemble some deceased relative, but this does not in any way indicate the reincarnation of an earlier child or relative. Again, we must say that this belief is not dealt with in Scripture. It is to be credited to Satan, who has invented such lies that deter men and women from believing the truth. In summary, we note that there is nothing in the Scriptures which permits any attempt to contact the spirits of the "living-dead." Mankind has a Saviour in Jesus Christ, who is the righteous judge of all who have died. These people are in his hands. Any attempt to reach that realm is of Satan and carries the penalty of death. Only the grace of God will be able to help the animists to turn from their ancestral connections as they turn to place their faith in Christ. There are many instances in the Scriptures of remembering the people of God with respect and gratitude. God commanded that we honor our father and mother (see Exod.20:12), but this has nothing at all to do with ancestor worship or necromancy.

The Transfiguration in Perspective

Teaching about Christ's transfiguration (see Matt. 17:1-13) may present a special problem, because Moses and Elijah appeared on the mountain with Jesus, Peter, James, and John. We must note briefly some significant factors that separate this event from any activity of a medium or any type of necromancy. These are:

1. The disciples were not afraid, according to Matthew. This indicates that the transfiguration was of God. When the disciples thought they saw a ghost walking on the water (even though it was Jesus) in Matt. 14:25-26, they were terrified of the ghost. On the mountain they were terrified only at the mighty voice and presence of God.

2. The identity of Moses and Elijah was revealed to the disciples, so they were both resurrected by the power of God. They were real enough for the offer of shelters to be made—as real as Jesus. This is an additional assurance of the resurrection when Jesus Christ returns.

3. Moses and Elijah were with God. They were not asleep in some place reserved for the dead. It was apparently a natural thing for them to be in the presence of God.

4. They had neither any message about the ancestors nor a message to the living from the deceased. One represented the law and one represented the prophets, so validity is given to all that God has said and done. Yet, they did not glorify themselves to the disciples—only Jesus was left with them.

Clarke speaks about this relationship. He says:

> The disciples wished to detain Moses and Elijah that they might hear them: But God shows that the law which had been in force, and the prophets which had prophesied, until now, must all give place to Jesus; and he alone must now be attended to, as the way, the truth, and the life; for no man could come unto the Father but through him.[34]

Jesus overshadows all that preceded him and we are to see him only as our guide.

1 Exod. 20:3-5.

2 Lev. 26:30.

3 Deut. 29:17.

4 Ezek. 37:23.

5 1 Cor. 8:4.

6 Ps. 115:4-7.

7 Deut. 32:16-17.

8 1 Cor. 10:19-21.

9 1 Thess. 1:9.

10 Rev. 9:20-21.

11 John 6:44.

12 Num. 35:30.

13 Lev. 19:18.

14 Matt. 5:43-44.

15 Clarke, *Clarke's Commentary*, 5:76.

16 Exod. 21:23-24.

17 Clarke, *Clarke's Commentary*, 1:412.

18 Rom. 12:19.

19 Matt. 16:27.

20 Oosthuizen, *Post-Christianity*, p. 86.

21 Lev. 20:6.

22 Deut. 18:11-12.

23 Ps. 88:11.

24 Rom. 8:5-6.

25 H. Orton Wiley, *Christian Theology*, 3 vols. (Kansas City: Beacon Hill Press of Kansas City, 1943), 3:213.

26 2 Cor. 5:8.

27 Luke 23:43.

28 Rom. 8:37-39.

29 Rev. 14:13.

30 John 15:15b.

31 2 Pet. 1:3.

32 John 3:4, 5, 6.

33 Heb. 9:27.

34 Clarke, *Clarke's Commentary*, 6:175.

10

SCRIPTURAL HOPE
FOR VICTORY
OVER SORCERY

The Scriptural references up to this point have been selected to
shed light on the truth about sorcery. These show that sorcery
is of Satan, it is deceit, it is connected intimately with idolatry,
revenge, and contacting the deceased—and all of these things are
condemned with the most severe penalties.

So, it must be asked, Is there any hope for the sorcery-bound
people? Once convinced that sorcery practices are evil, can one
turn from sorcery to God? Without hesitancy the answer must be
a resounding YES! We have already indicated that the first step in
the turning is conviction by the Holy Spirit that the teaching of the
Scriptures is correct in its revelation about God's position against
sorcery. Likewise, in the case of King Saul we saw that knowledge
or mental assent to scriptural facts without the conviction of the
Holy Spirit is impotent and useless.

In Malachi is found one of the most precious verses in the Old
Testament. As indicated by numerous verses above, God's own
people sinned often against him. Yet in a magnificent testimony
of his love he says to them:

> I the LORD do not change. So you, descendants of
> Jacob, are not destroyed. Ever since the time of your fore-
> fathers you have turned away from my decrees and have
> not kept them. Return to me, and I will return to you.[1]

This is the ageless invitation of a loving God who does not change. The practical working out of this among the people is illustrated by the experiences of King Manasseh and King Josiah in the Old Testament, also in the stories of the converted sorcerers and the girl freed from bondage in the New Testament.

Turning from Sorcery in the Old Testament

The story of King Manasseh can help the animistic peoples understand the whole picture of sorcery, including the turning from sorcery to God. The extensive list of Manasseh's sins should be very meaningful to them. The many variations and combinations of sorcery facing them are comparable to the plight of Manasseh. They should easily identify with his sins, his sentence, his turning, and his restitution.

Manasseh's sins are listed in 2 Chr. 33:3-9 as follows:

1. He rebuilt the high places his father Hezekiah had demolished. The high places were where people worshiped the pagan gods.

2. He built altars to the Baals. These were local fertility gods and God challenged their power with the prophet Elijah on Mount Carmel (see 1 Kgs. 18).

3. He made Asherah poles. These were for worshiping a goddess.

4. He bowed down to all the starry hosts and worshiped them. This sin of astrology probably came from Egypt.

5. He built altars to worship the stars in both courts of the temple. He thus desecrated the sacred place where God was to meet his people.

6. He sacrificed his sons in the fire. This was exactly what God forbade the people of Israel to do in Deut. 18:10.

7. He practiced sorcery, divination, and witchcraft.

8. He consulted mediums and spiritists.

9. He put a carved image in the temple. This is idolatry in the extreme.

10. He led the people of Judah and Jerusalem astray. He not only sinned, but as a leader he influenced a city and a nation toward sin.

Judgment followed when God sent the Assyrian army to defeat

Manasseh's army. King Manasseh was taken prisoner, had a hook put through his nose, and was bound with bronze shackles and taken to exile in Babylon. He, too, was driven from the land. There remained only death for the judgment to be complete. Could such a man with this list of sins and with judgment upon him turn to the LORD God of Israel?

The Scriptures tell us:

> In his distress he sought the favor of the LORD his God and humbled himself greatly before the God of his fathers. And when he prayed to him, the LORD was moved by his entreaty and listened to his plea; so he brought him back to Jerusalem and to his kingdom. Then Manasseh knew that the LORD is God.[2]

Timing is important in presenting this story to the sorcery-bound people which shows the possibility of leaving all sins behind. There must first be a complete understanding of the magnitude of their sin, to the point of genuine humiliation. It was the extreme distress of his circumstances that brought Manasseh to this point. Earlier we are told that "The LORD spoke to Manasseh and his people, but they paid no attention."[3] So engrossed were they in their sinning that the Word of God itself could not penetrate their hardened hearts. Manasseh came to his senses with a terrible shock, and perhaps it will take a similar shock to awaken people today to their spiritual condition as related to sorcery. The war crises that often flare up, the devastating economic conditions that befall many, or personal tragedy, all may be used of God to bring a receptiveness to the Word of God that will show them the desperate condition of their hearts. Then comes the humbling—the most difficult step for anyone in an animistic culture to take. As mentioned earlier, this goes against every natural tendency in any person—but especially in the animists. It will come only as God works his grace in their hearts. Then their spiritual eyes will be opened.

Concerning Manasseh, we cannot know what "humbled himself greatly" means, but it is certain that it included an acute sense of sinfulness, a conviction that he deserved only just punishment from God, along with a full realization that he had no other possible help—either within his own resources or from his idols. It was

only then he turned to God. His turning was from the most sub-
dued position imaginable.

Manasseh prayed. What did he pray? We do not know, but it
seems confession was an essential part. He had to repent and confess all those sins and admit his guilt in the whole matter to God.
He prayed from a contrite, broken heart. This we can be sure of
because "God was moved by his entreaty and listened to his plea."[4]
God does not listen to any other kind of prayer from a sinner.
Elsewhere in the Scriptures we read: "The sacrifices of God are a
broken spirit; / a broken and contrite heart, / O God, you will not
despise."[5] Also, "He mocks proud mockers / but gives grace to the
humble."[6] Manasseh's prayers were pleas, entreaties, and begging
from the depths of his heart.

God heard those sincere prayers and forgave him, and returned
him to his kingdom. God was faithful to restore him; and in the
act of God reaching out to him, Manasseh knew that the LORD is
God. Yes, there must be a turning from sorcery of all kinds back to
God. Manasseh did not stop there, however. He proceeded to
work at rebuilding (probably patching) the wall of Jerusalem, and
setting his kingdom in order as it should have been. Then with the
presence of God with him, he set about to perform a difficult task.
He destroyed all the sinful places and practices which he had led
the people to accept. The sincerity of his humbling of himself, of
his turning to God, and of his praying is proven by these public
acts. We note that he got rid of the foreign gods, removed the
image which he had placed in the temple, took out the altars built
to the gods in the temple, and threw them out of the city. Surely
this was a grand scale ocular demonstration for the public to see
what had taken place in his heart and also to see the power of the
LORD God over all gods. He also gave visual public testimony by
worshiping with fellowship (peace) and thank offerings on the
restored temple altar. He concluded by telling the people to serve
the one true God of Israel.

The entire incident related here concerning Manasseh bears
out perfectly the reliability of the Scriptures and the dependabili-
ty of God. In Leviticus this very situation was foreseen and provided for by God. God spoke of the possibility of Israel becoming
apostate and sinning so that God would have them taken captive
as judgment. He said:

But if they will confess their sins and the sins of their fathers...then when their uncircumcised hearts are humbled and they pay for their sin...I will not reject them or abhor them so as to destroy them completely, breaking my covenant with them.[7]

The sorcery-bound people must learn that God is just and they, like all others, will pay for their sin; but that sin can be forgiven and they can count on God to be faithful to all who turn to him on the proper basis. Through grace he can restore them to be as if they had never sinned.

Another lesson concerning the total impact of sorcery and related sins is noted in the offspring of the sinful Manasseh. His son, Amon, was a wicked king and he failed to humble himself before God like Manasseh did. Manasseh had set in motion such powerful forces of sin in Israel that he never did get the people (or his son) to turn to God with him. This is a tragic price of sin. When people begin to turn from sorcery, they must be warned of this tragedy, so that they can see that they may be victorious after turning and yet fail to convince others to repent.

Another illustration of how God works in a life is found in the story of Josiah, the one delight in Manasseh's family. He was only eight years old when he became king, but at the age of sixteen he began to seek God. After four years of seeking, he found God and began the reform which his father, Amon, did not want to do and his grandfather, Manasseh, could not do. He purged Judah and Jerusalem and put the temple in order. In doing that, Hilkiah the priest found the book of the Law of Moses. This had apparently been put aside, either carelessly, or purposefully to preserve it, because no one knew what it said. When it was read to King Josiah he was terrified, realizing they were all operating without God's Word to guide them. Immediately the king sought to inquire of the LORD to know what to do about God's righteous anger against them. God told him:

Because your heart was responsive and you humbled yourself before God when you heard what he spoke against this place and its people, and because you humbled yourself before me and tore your robes and wept in my presence, I have heard you....[8]

When Josiah humbled himself before God, he not only saved himself but also the entire nation. God said that (according to justice) the nation would pay for their turning away from God—but not until Josiah's reign was finished. In heeding and following God's Word, the king found life for a nation throughout the thirty-one years of his reign. Each animistic person who repents is just as precious as the others, but first the ministry should, where possible, be directed toward the leaders. This can be done naturally because the leaders usually show some interest in the church and its ministry. One obedient leader can influence an entire nation.

New Testament Illustrations

Regardless of how helpful the Old Testament is for understanding sorcery, it must always be presented as the forerunner of the New Testament. The African people love the Old Testament because it is so descriptive of their own situation. However, the increasing numbers of independent African churches and the lack of spiritual victory in the historical churches indicates that many never move from the Old Testament to the New Testament. Whenever one teaches from the Old Testament, it must be clearly related to Jesus Christ of the New Testament. The first two verses of Hebrews, chapter one, should be used as a constant reminder (even a motto) of the relationship of the two. These verses state:

> In the past God spoke to our forefathers (in Israel) through the prophets at many times and in various ways, but in these last days he has spoken to us by his Son, whom he appointed heir of all things, and through whom he made the universe.[9]

There is to be no contemplation of victory outside of Jesus Christ and the infilling of the Holy Spirit!

In Acts we encounter two other instances of sorcery confrontation. The first is a girl who practiced fortune-telling or divining. The Scriptures tell us that this slave girl "had a spirit by which she predicted the future. She earned a great deal of money for her owners by fortune-telling." There is no doubt that she was practicing what is classed here as sorcery, but in this case she had a spirit—she was possessed by it. Her spirit was the manifestation of Satan or one of his demons, and he caused her to cry out as she followed Paul, Silas, Luke, and the other Christians who were on their way to pray. She shouted after them for days, crying: "These men are servants of the Most High God, who are telling you the way to be saved."[10]

The statement was true, and it came from Satan (or his demon). This shows the cunning of the deceit of Satan. By telling the truth, everyone who heard the girl would suppose that the Christians were part of the pagan system, so no one would need to listen to them—they had nothing new. Also, the unconverted Jews would then connect the Christians with the group of sorcerers. This would discredit the Christians, because the Jews by law were not allowed to have any dealings with sorcery or diviners, etc. Thus, Satan was extremely clever in his attempt to discredit the Christians by telling the truth.

Then the Scriptures continue:

> Finally Paul became so troubled that he turned around and said to the spirit, "In the name of Jesus Christ I command you to come out of her!" At that moment the spirit left her.[11]

There was no turning to God, there was no confession of sin, no praying on her part. Through the power of the risen Christ, Paul was able to cast the demon out. Christ's power was completely superior to the power of the demon. However, we do not see the girl finding salvation or following the Lord even after what she experienced.

Paul did not act hastily. The girl tormented them for days before he cast the spirit out. Today any successful ministry to the sorcery-bound people will be accomplished by those who walk in spiritual victory and who know the power of the Holy Spirit within themselves. They, like Paul, will need it for two main reasons: first, to have the wisdom and discernment to know how Satan is involved with a particular person or situation; second, to have the power over all that Satan possesses. But as we consider the whole event we see a third reason for having the presence of the Holy Spirit. The men were angry because the girl could no longer tell fortunes for them, so they began an enormous amount of trouble, causing Paul and Silas to be stripped, flogged, and thrown into the inner jail. As one ministers against sorcery and its many related sins, people affected adversely by that ministry will cause trouble. If the dungeon doors clink shut and the sores throb, that is the time to pray and sing—by the power of the Holy Spirit!

Another story in Acts relates that some Jews tried to cast out demons in the name of the Lord Jesus Christ without knowing him as Saviour and without the power of the Holy Spirit. We read: "They would say, 'In the name of Jesus whom Paul preaches, I command you to come out.'" There were seven of them doing this, but the Scripture relates:

> The evil spirit answered them, "Jesus I know and Paul I know about, but who are you?" Then the man who had the evil spirit jumped on them and overpowered them all. He gave them such a beating that they ran out of the house naked and bleeding.[12]

No victory in Jesus, and no power of the Holy Spirit, spells no success when working against the wiles and powers of Satan. Satan and his evil spirits recognize a powerless impostor who comes falsely in the name of Jesus. Anyone can expect troubles from Satan when they try to resist sorcery or those who are under Satan's spirit power. These impostors were beaten up and the genuine Christians above were also beaten and put in jail.

The Lord is able to take such difficult and adverse situations and bring praise to his name! This even happened when the impostors were beaten up, for the word of that encounter got around Ephesus, so that "they were all seized with fear and the name of the Lord Jesus was held in high honor."[13] The reason for the high honor was that it was obvious that only Jesus Christ had the power to deal with the spirits. It also served to openly reveal to the people what sort of violent spirits Satan uses. They were afraid to be impostors and, thus, have no power, they were afraid of the satanic powers, and they were afraid of the Jesus whom even the evil spirits could identify. In the Bible we continue to read:

Many of those who believed now came and openly confessed their evil deeds. A number who had practiced sorcery brought their scrolls together and burned them publicly. When they calculated the value of the scrolls, the total came to fifty thousand drachmas.(One drachma was about one day's wage.) In this way the word of the Lord spread widely and grew in power.[14]

There must be public confession, because there is nothing genuine if the convert is hiding his faith in Jesus Christ. Some tried that, but it resulted in fear. They had held back, so there was no victory. When the articles connected with their sorcery were brought to be burned publicly, then they were able to find victory. The high value of the objects burned indicates the sincerity of their turning to God. The public fire was a testimony to others, an ocular demonstration, and served as an inner witness, too. Such a testimony has the effect of establishing a new faith so it is more certain. The Lord used all aspects of the impostors' attempt to cast out demons in the name of Jesus, as well as the genuine turning to him by those who burned their sorcery books, so that "In this way the word of the Lord spread widely and grew in power."[15]

Demons/Evil Spirits as Related to Sorcery

Demon/evil spirit possession occurs even today. Anyone who would minister effectively must believe this and be Biblically and spiritually prepared to deal with it. Just as in the above story in Acts, sorcery and possession by evil spirits often meet and become a complex problem.

In Southern Congo a secondary school student bought "medicines" from a sorcerer to help his grades and to increase his sexual power over the girls. As a result, according to his own testimony, he became possessed by evil spirits, which eventually rendered him dumb and mentally incapacitated. In desperation his family brought him to the missionary school principal to request help. Four Congolese pastors were summoned, and following an hour of prayer the evil spirits were cast out in the name of Jesus Christ. The young man regained his right mind, along with his speech, and accepted Jesus Christ as his Saviour right then.

As in scriptural accounts, Satan uses an endless assortment of

129

combinations to confuse, conquer and destroy people. Sin makes them susceptible, vulnerable victims. However, it is for all such victims that Jesus Christ went to the cross and gained victory over all that Satan has in his arsenal!

One word of caution is needed concerning demons/evil spirits. Since the spirit world is so real and so inclusive to animistic peoples, Satan may be given more credit than necessary as concerns possession. Not all physical illness, not all psychological disturbances, are caused by possession by evil spirits. It is easy to see demons everywhere, causing everything that is evil. Again, the Scriptures show us that discernment is needed to know when this is a problem, and when it is confirmed to know that the power of the Holy Spirit is more than adequate to deal with it.

In conclusion, the entire Bible is the base for any ministry to sorcery-bound people. Both the Old and New Testaments reveal truth and offer countless illustrations to show how God works, how Satan acts, and how people are trapped in sorcery—except by the victory of Jesus Christ and the power of the Holy Spirit. The Bible exposes the truth about sin and opens the door of hope to all who seek God's face aright.

---

[1] Mal. 3:6-7.

[2] 2 Chr. 33:12-13.

[3] 2 Chr. 33:10.

[4] 2 Chr. 33:13.

[5] Ps. 51:17.

[6] Prov. 3:34; Jas. 4:6; 1 Pet. 5:5.

[7] Lev. 26:40-45.

[8] 2 Chr. 34:27.

[9] Heb. 1:1-2.

10 Acts 16:16, 17.

11 Acts 16:18.

12 Acts 19:13, 14-16.

13 Acts 19:17.

14 Acts 19:18-20.

15 Acts 19:20.

11

GAINING SPIRITUAL VICTORY OVER SORCERY

The downward thrust of the Scriptures upon the sinner, as outlined in the previous chapter, reveals the sinfulness of sorcery and eventually illumines the soul, thus bringing conviction. This entire process must be taught to the animist who is trapped in sorcery, in order to avoid skimming toward a false victory. There is no short-cut; people cannot do what time with the Scriptures and the Holy Spirit must do. The penalty for sorcery is death, and we shall assume at this point that that realization has been grasped by the sinner through the grace of God.

Personal Responsibility and Choice

The next step, which is a part of the turning to God, is the realization by the sinner that the choice is personal. The convicted person looks both directions and finally admits, "Yes, it is I who have sinned!" Then that person must be led to make a personal choice. Among animists this is extremely difficult. They remember their fatalistic philosophy which declares: "Nothing you do will really matter in the end." Their cultural ethic cries out: "Don't divulge your secrets; don't expose your soul—or else!" So with clarity and persistence the Scriptures must be taught to them, so that they will be able to build a reasonable and accurate base for decision.

God could have chosen to create robots instead of free people. Since he did not, but rather chose to create man with the ability to think, to reason, and to choose, God's desire is for man to choose to be his completely. The ability to choose permits a person to develop one's own capabilities. However, people were not created to function properly without choosing God's way. God's plan is the best for all people, and it is the only plan that leads to eternal life with him. Consequently, it is God's will for everyone to choose life; but the choice is up to each person.

There is a popular idea among African animists that God is the source of evil <u>because</u> he gave man this choice. They have the idea that the power to choose <u>caused</u> them to fall into sin—it is God's fault. Many overlook the fact that humankind was already on one way, the way that leads to death, when God in his love and concern added the second way to life through faith in Jesus Christ.

However, the wisdom of Jesus is practical and must be taught to correct this erroneous thinking. Paul is very clear on this point as well. He tells the Thessalonians: "It is God's will that you should be holy...."[1] Therefore, God could not be the cause of evil if his will for man is to be just the opposite of evil.

Old Testament Choices

Throughout the Old Testament there are constant reminders of the gift of choice which God has given. Adam and Eve were given a choice. By disobeying God they chose the way of sin and death. This is stated clearly in God's offer to the Israelites before they were to enter Canaan. God declared: .

> This day I call heaven and earth as witnesses against you that I have set before you life and death, blessings and curses. Now choose life, so that you and your children may live and that you may love the LORD your God, listen to his voice, and hold fast to him. For the LORD is your life...[2]

It seems likely that after being delivered from slavery, following the Deliverer would be a reasonable choice. But Satan deceived the Israelites, just as he has deceived all of mankind since then. Thus, the Israelites turned from God and began to worship idols. The false promises of sin tempted them away to idolatry, sorcery, and countless other abominable practices. That first choice offered life or death; so when the Israelites chose sin they also chose judgment and death.

Then Joshua came before those sinful Israelites and repeated the offer of a choice. He urged them, saying:

Now fear the Lord and serve him with all faithfulness. Throw away the gods of your forefathers worshiped beyond the River in Egypt, and serve the LORD. But if serving the Lord seems undesireable to you, then choose for yourselves this day whom you will serve....[3]

The people were not coerced into following God—the choice was theirs. They had a responsibility to make a choice and then to accept the consequences of that choice. They did not have to choose blindly, because God told them in advance the results of each choice. In this case, they chose to serve the LORD. They wanted to enter the promised land. Also, the desert experience was fresh on their minds, so without hesitancy they chose to serve the LORD. This choice made in Joshua's time did not last, and later the Israelites fell into deep sin repeatedly.

The prophet Elijah also placed the same choice before the people. On Mount Carmel he cried out: "How long will you waver between two opinions? If the LORD is God, follow him; but if Baal is God, follow him."[4] Instead of answering that they would follow the LORD, as with Joshua, the people just stood there. By this time they were into sorcery and all the sins of Canaan, plus some extras—they didn't choose God quickly. They were far enough into sin that they couldn't choose quickly. It wasn't until Elijah called fire from heaven, in the name of the LORD God, in a contest with the prophets of Baal that they finally saw the light. In this contest God answered Elijah's prayer. The Israelites saw and believed.

These and other Old Testament lessons concerning choice must be taught to the animistic people who wish to be free from sorcery. There is no way to be free from sorcery except in choosing to turn from it and deliberately choosing to accept God on his terms. His terms are in the Scriptures and we all must turn to them.

New Testament Choices

In the New Testament Jesus also taught about the necessity to choose. He pointed out:

No servant can serve two masters. Either he will hate the one and love the other, or he will be devoted to the one and despise the other. You cannot serve God and Money.[5]

135

He could have said, "God and sorcery" or "God and idols" or any such thing. The point here is that a person cannot possibly divide the affection of his heart. Individuals must make a choice between God and whatever else might be substituted in his place.

In Thessalonians, the choice and the results of the choice are stated negatively by Paul: "Therefore, he who rejects that instruction does not reject man but God...."[6] This concept can be used to encourage the animistic people to accept (that is choose) the instructions of God, as they are found in his Word.

Peter teaches a similar truth which includes choice. He states: "...He is patient with you, not wanting anyone to perish, but everyone to come to repentance."[7] Here a long-suffering God is revealed who in his infinite love wills no person to be lost. If evil is the cause for people's perishing, he cannot be the author of evil, because he desires all people to repent and come to him for eternal life.

We find a sad story in Matthew that convinces us of the perfect freedom to choose. Jesus cast the demons out of two violent men and made the demons go into a herd of pigs. When the pigs ran down to the lake and drowned, the people tending them ran to tell the villagers all about it. The Scriptures add: "Then the whole town went out to see Jesus. And when they saw him, they pleaded with him to leave their region."[8] Two violent men were made whole that day. The village could have seen other miracles if they had chosen to receive Jesus. Most people chose to hear him and to seek his favor and help; however, this village made the opposite choice. They chose definitely and surely to ask him to <u>leave</u>. They lost their big chance, and Jesus permitted them to exercise that freedom of will—he left them!

A Congolese Christian (a former animist) refused a request by a distraught mother to pray for her possessed daughter. The reason he gave for the refusal revealed discernment on his part when he said: "She has already made her choice." The girl had been to a sorcerer who cast out several evil spirits, but permitted her to choose to keep three spirits who indicated they would be helpful. Choice, then, is given to all people, but it needs to be related to the best choice of all, that provided in Jesus Christ by the love of God the Father.

The imperatives or commands in the Scriptures also imply that the hearer should choose to turn to God and be obedient. When Jesus says: "...unless you repent, you too will all perish,"[9] he implies that there is a choice, and that it is urgent to choose to repent. There is the pronouncement of judgment to clarify the situation, but no coercion. When Jesus urges: "Seek first his kingdom and his righteousness,"[10] he is admonishing his hearers to make the choice to seek God's kingdom first before all other things, but he leaves that decision up to them.

These Scriptural references and inferences leave no doubt about the personal responsibility in choice, and, thus, the personal responsibility in the final destiny of each person. Wherever the animists' culture does not agree with the above truths, there must be a careful correction made on the basis of the nature of God as it is revealed in the Scriptures. In addition, the animists need to realize that all peoples lack adequate knowledge of God without the Scriptures, therefore, in adjusting any beliefs to conform to the Bible, they are joining many others from other cultures who have also turned to God.

The Process of Choosing God

Once the process is clearly understood up to this point, a person is ready to turn to God. It will suddenly occur to the seekers that they are perishing, and through the work of the Holy Spirit in their heart they will make the choice to turn to God—only to discover that a sinner is separated from the Holy God. This must be resolved for the animist in a concrete way, step by step with the Scriptures.

The Sin Offering

In the Law of Moses God declared that sin is so evil it brings death; therefore, the only way sin can be atoned for is in the sacrifice of life. He said: "For the life of a creature is in the blood, and I have given it to you to make atonement for yourselves on the altar; it is the blood that makes atonement for one's life."[11] In Hebrews we read: "In fact, the law requires that nearly everything be cleansed with blood, and without the shedding of blood there is no forgiveness."[12] The death of the sacrificed animal was substituted for the just death of the person who had sinned before God. The Old Testament meaning is to cover the sins of the person making the sacrifice (or offering) to God.

The traditional culture of the animists includes the sacrifice of animals, and in some instances it includes the pouring of blood over a fetish or idol in order to obtain some benefit from the god or spirit it represents. The sacrifices of the Old Testament will undoubtedly be compared to these; but even though there is a definite relationship, they must be carefully delineated. The atonement (or expiation) for the sins of people, as commanded in the Law of Moses, is necessary because of the righteous judgment of a Holy God. There is no manipulation or magic involved. The animal offered for sin was to be a perfect beast with no blemish of any kind. The atonement for sin required the death of their best animal. Unless these points are carefully contrasted with each local practice of sacrifice, the animist may become confused. Any such lack of clarity will lessen the significance of the sin sacrifice and lower the perceived position of the Holy and Just God.

Transition to Jesus Christ as our Sin Offering

The animist who seeks to approach God must now be guided past the sin offerings of the law and on to faith in Jesus Christ. Hebrews is the most pertinent book in the New Testament for making this transition. In the first two verses we read of the change to the new covenant:

> In the past God spoke to our forefathers through the prophets at many times and various ways, but in these last days he has spoken to us by his Son whom he appointed heir of all things and through whom he made the universe.[13]

This establishes Jesus Christ as the Son of God through whom God created all things. As such, he is the only valid one to show us what God is saying to people today. The law and the prophets are all fulfilled in Jesus, so we are to shift our attention from the sacrifice of animals to him and to his work on the cross. The following verse introduces that accomplished work:

> The Son is the radiance of God's glory and the exact representation of his being, sustaining all things by his

138

powerful word. After he had provided purification for sins, he sat down at the right hand of the Majesty of heaven.[14]

The divinity of Jesus is proclaimed here along with his work.

The picture of Jesus as our sin offering is developed throughout the book of Hebrews in terms that are relevant to the animists. In chapter two we find the humanity of Christ upheld: "Since the children have flesh and blood, he too shared in their humanity so that by his death he might destroy him who holds the power of death—that is, the devil...."[15] This removes Christ from the mystical realm of the spirits where contact is never quite obtainable. Though he was God, he was also a person to whom all peoples can relate.

In the following verses Jesus is shown to be the great high priest of all mankind: "Therefore since we have a great high priest who has gone through the heavens, Jesus the Son of God, let us hold firmly to the faith we profess."[16] To the animist, the one making the offering is very significant. He is considered to be powerful and is expected to perform all of his rituals with care. In many passages the author of Hebrews makes the position of Christ clear and relates it to God, to the Old Testament, and to all people everywhere. He writes: "But when this priest had offered for all time one sacrifice for sins, he sat down at the right hand of God."[17] This verse is eternally inclusive for each person today, even as it was in the New Testament times. It must be noted that faith in Jesus Christ is the qualifier—there is no place for universalism (i.e. all people are saved automatically).

As these important themes in Hebrews are taught, other Scriptures can be introduced to further develop any of the important doctrines. For example, the love of God which sent his Son to save us can easily be introduced. The third chapter of John can add that dimension to the Sacrificial High Priest. In like manner, the voluntary nature of his sacrifice will show the dimension of love. Speaking of his own life, Jesus said: "No one takes it from me, but I lay it down of my own accord. I have authority to lay it down and authority to take it up again."[18] Jesus, according to the perfect will of God, was the sacrifice for the whole world because he chose to do that which would provide a way to obtain life for many. These correlations develop an understanding of the magnitude of what Christ did for us on the cross.

Hebrews, then, can be considered a basic book for helping the animists make the transition from the Old Testament to the New Testament and thus to Jesus Christ. The seekers can see by the grace of the Holy Spirit that Jesus is the adequate sacrifice and the promised Saviour. The many comparisons to the Old Testament law help to give a concrete picture of the unique place which Jesus Christ occupies as Saviour of the world.

God's Gift of Salvation

Perhaps the most difficult concept to understand about salvation is that God has given all of salvation free of charge. This is particularly difficult for the animists to comprehend. They are not accustomed to free gifts of any kind in their world of living spirits. In that system gifts may be given simply to establish a relationship between two people, or to close a deal of any kind. Again, gifts may be used to obligate another person. This happens when a wife is given to a chief by any of his subjects or by a clan. The chief is then obligated to hear their complaints or requests. In a similar sense, gifts are given in order to gain favor or to obtain good fortune. The gifts, if approved by the spirits, would enhance the prospects of the giver in that case. Gifts have strings attached in the animistic world and the ulterior motives of the giver make it difficult for animists to understand the reality of a free gift.

Paul speaks of the gift of God and the grace of God many times, and often they are spoken of together. By the working of the Holy Spirit through God's Word these truths can be substituted for the disappointing concept of gifts held by the animists. Paul says:

> The gift is not like the trespass. For if the many died by the trespass of the one man, how much more did God's grace and the gift that came by the grace of the one man, Jesus Christ, overflow to the many![19]

Unmerited, undeserved and unearned grace is operating in salvation through Jesus Christ. No man planned for salvation through a Saviour; it was God's plan because of his love. It is too profound and too vast for one person to be able to pay for his part in it. Later Paul says: "For the wages of sin is death, but the gift of God is eternal life in Christ Jesus our Lord."[20] Salvation not only involves our present situation and bondage, but it also involves life eternal—with God.

Because of the people's concept of gifts, animists will be tempted to believe that salvation is a free gift only because the cost of forgiveness, a new birth, and eternal life is so enormous that no one could collect that much (even among relatives). In a sense this is true; however, the Scriptures show that salvation is a result of God's love and not the result of our inability to pay. Even though the saved are considered to be slaves of God instead of slaves to sin (see Rom. 6:22), and even though they are saved to do good works which God prepared for them to do (see Eph. 2:10), these are not counted as payments for their salvation. In fact, we read: "For it is by grace you have been saved, through faith—and this not from yourselves, it is the gift of God—not by works, so that no one can boast."[21]

Wiley quotes Adam Clarke concerning God's grace and faith. In this quote Clarke helps us to reconcile this gift of God and the previously mentioned element of personal choice by explaining:

> "Is not faith the gift of God? Yes, as to the grace by which it is produced; but the grace or power to believe, and the act of believing are two different things. Without the grace or power to believe no man ever did or can believe; but with that power the act of faith is a man's own. God never believes for any man, no more than He repents for him; the penitent, through this grace enabling him, believes for himself....This, therefore, is the true state of the case: God gives the power, man uses the power thus given, and brings glory to God: Without the power no man can believe; with it, any man may."

> (cf. Clarke, Ch. The., pp. 135, 136. Also <u>Commentary,</u> Heb. 11:1).[22]

It is by God's grace and the teaching of the Scriptures that any animists can come to perceive the unspeakable gift of salvation in Jesus Christ and yet, at the same time, accept their responsibility in the act of true repentance and in choosing to trust in saving faith. Without this dual emphasis, there is danger that the seekers will want salvation but expect God to coerce them into faith. Their traditional fatalism would expect that. Then any failure to grow, to bear fruit for the kingdom of God, or to do good works would be conveniently blamed on God.

Regardless of the problems involved or the speed of the progress toward Jesus Christ, the teaching of these basic Scriptures must never replace or hide the moment of decision, when the turning is complete, the gospel understood, and faith declared. This may come at any point along the line of progress, and will become an essential reference point for all subsequent decisions and growth.

---

[1] 1 Thess. 4:3.

[2] Deut. 30:19-20.

[3] Josh. 24:14-15.

[4] 1 Kgs. 18:20.

[5] Luke 16:13.

[6] 1 Thess. 4:7.

[7] 2 Pet. 3:9.

[8] Matt. 8:34.

[9] Luke 13:3.

[10] Matt. 6:33.

[11] Lev. 17:11.

[12] Heb. 9:22.

13 Heb. 1:1-2.

14 Heb. 1:3.

15 Heb. 2:14.

16 Heb. 4:14.

17 Heb. 10:12.

18 John 10:18.

19 Rom. 5:15.

20 Rom. 6:23.

21 Eph. 2:8-9.

22 Wiley, *Christian Theology*, 2:369, 370.

12

SCRIPTURAL
PROMISES FOR
THE REPENTANT SOUL

When a person chooses to turn to God, and the Holy Spirit is working in his heart, God's Word has many precious promises to encourage him. The testimony of Peter explains this so well. He declares:

> His divine power has given us everything we need for life and godliness through our knowledge of him who called us by his own glory and goodness. Through these he has given us his very great and precious promises, so that through them you may participate in the divine nature and escape the corruption in the world caused by evil desires.[1]

God's promises include forgiveness, freedom, and the promises of assurance.

The Promises of Forgiveness

True repentance includes an awareness of guilt and of sins committed against God. As one turns to God for mercy what will he find? It will be tragic if the missionary, or the pastor, or a Christian friend are seen. The seekers need to see the Word and all it says to encourage them about believing in Jesus Christ.

One also needs to know that all of heaven looks forward to their moment of faith. Jesus said: "In the same way, I tell you, there is rejoicing in the presence of the angels of God over one sinner who repents."[2] The struggle is not unnoticed if the struggle is toward God. In this same chapter Jesus uses the parables of the lost sheep, the lost coin, and the lost son to teach that a repentant person will be received with forgiveness and joy.

Another view of forgiveness is seen when Paul assures the Corinthians that sinners cannot inherit the kingdom of God. He says:

> Do not be deceived: Neither the sexually immoral nor idolators nor adulterers nor male prostitutes nor homosexual offenders nor thieves nor the greedy nor drunkards nor slanderers nor swindlers will inherit the kingdom of God.[3]

This is a formidable list of sins and some will be very pertinent to the animist trapped in sorcery. These verses must not be separated from the one which follows, or despair will overcome the repentant person. Paul continues: "And that is what some of you were. But you were washed, you were sanctified, you were justified in the name of the Lord Jesus Christ and by the Spirit of our God."[4]

The point is not despair, but victory. If some of the Corinthian Christians were included in that list of sins, but had since been washed (that is forgiven), and even justified (counted as if they had never sinned), then there is certainly hope for the animist who turns toward God and asks for mercy! That person, too, will be accepted, forgiven, justified, and sanctified.

John also speaks of the forgiveness of sins, but in yet another way. He says: "Everyone who sins breaks the law; in fact sin is lawlessness. But you know that he appeared so that he might take away our sins. And in him is no sin."[5] This taking away of our sins should be meaningful to the penitent animist if forgiveness is difficult to understand. The forgiveness experienced in the local traditions is quite shallow, and may have an element of "getting by" in it. However, both John and Paul make it plain that there is no getting by with only part of one's sins forgiven. Hence, the concept of the removal of sins may be especially helpful to the animist.

These references in the New Testament all point to the consistency of God. From the beginning he has sought people who would repent of their sin and turn to him. In Leviticus God declares: "...the priest will make atonement for them, and they will be forgiven."[6] This was true for the people of Israel as a community and for individuals as well. Whenever atonement was made, forgiveness was assured. Undoubtedly this atoning required the repentance essential for forgiveness, as it is more clearly stated in 2 Chronicles. In this book we read:

> ...if my people, who are called by my name, will humble themselves and pray and seek my face and turn from their wicked ways, then will I hear from heaven and will forgive their sin and will heal their land.[7]

Whenever people turn to God in true repentance he is willing to receive them.

The difference in the Old Covenant and the New Covenant as concerns the forgiveness of sins is not in the nature of God, but in the nature of the sacrifice. The author of Hebrews states that the animals sacrificed under the Old Covenant accomplished their purpose and adds:

> How much more, then, will the blood of Christ who through the eternal Spirit offered himself unblemished to God, cleanse our consciences from acts that lead to death, so that we may serve the living God.[8]

The heavy conscience of the animist may be cleansed from all the sin that leads to death—the Scriptures teach us that promise!

The Promises of Release

The forgiveness of sins is important and an essential part of salvation, but it is not the most urgent of the questions pressing in on the repentant animist. The most important question must be, Is there release and true freedom from sorcery for me? Speaking to Jews who were in bondage to sin, Jesus said: "If you hold to my teaching, you are really my disciples. Then you will know the truth and the truth will set you free." Later, in the same discussion, he spoke to them about his unique relationship as the Son to the Father. He declared: "So if the Son sets you free, you will be free indeed."[9] Jesus said these things to people who were children of the devil, in bondage to him. So great was their bondage that they believed all the devil's lies and actually belonged to him, even as sorcery-bound people are his also. This bondage to Satan prevented the Jews from understanding the truth that Jesus was trying to reveal to them, therefore, many rejected Jesus. The devil was their choice. However, Jesus made it very clear in the above passages that freedom from this bondage is available. It is found only in him as the Son of God, in the truth that is available in his teachings (his Word), and in the power of the Holy Spirit.

Paul also speaks of freedom from sin and rejoices in the news about the Thessalonians when he writes:

> They tell how you turned to God from idols to serve the living and true God, and to wait for his Son from heaven, whom he raised from the dead—Jesus, who rescues us from the coming wrath.[10]

Here the animist finds precedent in those who were worshiping idols, yet who, by God's grace in Jesus Christ, were rescued from the death due to sinners. Here is hope that can be specifically applied to the sorcery problem, along with Jesus' declarations mentioned above.

Another passage that is helpful in the consideration of freedom is actually part of Paul's own testimony. He exclaims:

> Therefore, there is now no condemnation for those who are in Christ Jesus, because through Christ Jesus the law of the Spirit of life set me free from the law of sin and death.[11]

Paul did not need to be set free from the bondage of sorcery, but from the bondage of the Law. As a trained Jew he was in bondage to all the sacrifices and practices that were a part of the Mosaic Law. He found that the Law did not change his inner self and that he was powerless to free himself from the fruitless struggle. In this struggle he had much in common with the people bound by sorcery—no human effort is of any avail. The freedom comes through Christ Jesus who makes possible a new law of the Spirit of life (see

Rom. 6:18 and Gal. 5:1).

In Hebrews we find a different freedom mentioned which is important. The author explains:

> Since the children have flesh and blood, he too shared in their humanity so that by his death he might destroy him who holds the power of death— that is, the devil—and free those who all their lives were held in slavery by their fear of death.[12]

Here we have not only a statement of the humanity of Jesus Christ but we have the defeat of Satan. The animist who repents must have a keen awareness of the power of Satan and his ability to deceive people throughout their lifetime. The fear generated by the devil's work is devastating and is well known. That fear brings slavery and bondage, so the promise to be set free from that is extremely important. We can conclude this section with Paul's words: "The sting of death is sin, and the power of sin is the law. But thanks be to God! He gives us the victory through our Lord Jesus Christ."[13]

The Promises of Assurance

All who come to God through faith in Jesus Christ will sooner or later wonder if they can know when they have passed from death to life, from unbelief to faith. Animists, too, will need much assurance from the Scriptures, because they are surrounded by people and objects that remind them of their past defeat. The promises of assurance will encourage the new Christian to press on in victory because they are so definite. They center in God the Father, God the Holy Spirit, and God the Son.

One part of the believer's assurance comes from God's desire to make clear his unchangeable plan. In order to give believers confidence in the continuity of salvation, God promised Abraham that he would be blessed and have many descendants. To that promise he added an oath by swearing by himself. Paul explains:

> God did this so that, by two unchangeable things in which it is impossible for God to lie, we who have fled to take hold of the hope offered to us may be greatly encour-

aged. We have this hope as an anchor for the soul, firm and secure.[14]

This great encouragement comes from God himself and is passive because the covenant has already been established. He does not want believers to be insecure because they think he might change his mind. The hope we have in the covenant with him through Jesus Christ is firm and nothing can ever shake it.

The animist who has faced constant change and has lacked any absolutes may find this assurance too much to believe. Therefore, the statement that we have fled to take hold of the hope gives one a contact with the actual situation. Having fled sorcery, something terrible and very real, in repentance one now reaches out to grab the hope which God alone offers, much like a drowning person clings to a rope. Once people see themselves included in this passage in Hebrews, then the guarantee or promise that the "rope" can be completely trusted will bring much comfort and encouragement. The animists can also recognize their God, because, traditionally, their concept of God portrays him as unchangeable. These are definite cultural bridge points.

As sorcery-bound people reach out in faith to Jesus Christ as Saviour, those who minister to them should point out how clearly the Scriptures portray Jesus as their perfectly adequate Redeemer. Jesus is completely capable of handling the sorcery problem and of saving them. John tells us, "The reason the Son of God appeared was to destroy the devil's work."[15] God's love, the reason; the all powerful Jesus, the destroyer; the devil, who has been working—all of these are pertinent!

This Jesus can be trusted because "having disarmed the powers and authorities, he made a public spectacle of them, triumphing over them by the cross."[16] He is the Christ, "...who is the head over every power and authority."[17] He is, then, the superior power, over all sorcery and satanic powers of all kinds! This is why in God's Word he declares boldly, "So if the Son sets you free, you will be free indeed."[18] Jesus lives today, he is the one ". . . who has gone into heaven and is at God's right hand—with angels, authorities and powers in submission to him."[19] Jesus states that the prince of this world, that is Satan, "...has no hold on me."[20]

Every assurance is given to those who trust this victorious

Christ. Not only was that victory gained at the cross and through the resurrection, it is also operative and relevant to those who fear the powers of sorcery as they trust in him to save them now and throughout eternity. As believers, Jesus refers to them as his sheep, saying:

> My sheep listen to my voice; I know them, and they follow me. I give them eternal life, and they shall never perish; no one can snatch them out of my hand. My Father who has given them to me is greater than all; no one can snatch them out of my Father's hand. I and the Father are one.[21]

The Guarantee

Believers can count on him without being disappointed. The apostle Paul, who learned to trust Jesus completely in all circumstances, writes: "But the Lord is faithful, he will strengthen and protect you from the evil one."[22] In another book he also states: "He will keep you strong to the end, so that you will be blameless on the day of our Lord Jesus Christ. God, who has called you into his fellowship with his Son Jesus Christ our Lord, is faithful."[23] This faithful God is Good News for anyone fleeing sorcery.

The eternal nature of the guarantee is also based on Jesus Christ, the resurrected, eternal high priest. Paul adds: "He has become a high priest forever...,"[24] and later says: "Because of this oath, Jesus has become the guarantee of a better covenant."[25] Jesus, then, is the object of our hope, and because he is risen his guarantee is for eternity. There can be no greater assurance offered to those who seek to reach out for God's plan of salvation than these two guarantees from the Father and the Son.

Another more active part of the believer's assurance is found in Paul's second letter to the Corinthians. He declares:

> Now it is God who makes both us and you stand firm in Christ. He anointed us, set his seal of ownership on us, and put his Spirit in our hearts as a deposit, guaranteeing what is to come.[26]

God's strengthening causes us to stand firm as believers. We are as his slaves, bought with the precious price of the blood of Jesus Christ. Since slavery is recent enough history to be vividly recalled, then this new relationship with God the Father is understandable in that light. The teaching must include the fact that this Father is the perfect Master who purchased us out of love and bought life for us. At the same time, that picture can be balanced with the truth that we are children (in another sense). We are declared to be: "...heirs of God and co-heirs with Christ...."[27] This is shown, too, by the anointing mentioned in 2 Cor. 1:21 above. As co-heirs we are to reign with Christ in his kingdom, so the idea that God has bought us is a very positive concept when viewed in perspective.

At the same time, we have the Holy Spirit within our hearts as a pledge of what God has for us in the future. Jesus promised to send the Holy Spirit and called him the Counselor and the Spirit of truth. This implies the Holy Spirit's active participation in the believer's life as a helper and guide. Speaking of the Holy Spirit, Jesus declares: "But you know him, for he lives with you and will be in you. I will not leave you as orphans; I will come to you."[28] This is the promise of his indwelling the believer with his Spirit, the Holy Spirit of God.

In contrast, animists worship fetishes or idols. The idols are external and usually placed in some designated spot. They are only accessible in that spot, just as sorcery is located only with the practitioner or the client. Thus, we can clearly define the contrast of the abiding Spirit of God within us—at all times and in all places. In a real sense a Christian is possessed by the Holy Spirit. Evil spirits and demons possess some people who are not Christians. Possession by the Spirit of the Living God may be compared and contrasted with local beliefs and customs, but only in the light of scriptural teaching.

The fact that God occupies our hearts does not remove the personal responsibility of keeping the faith, but it does mean that we have new guidance, new desires, and new incentives within us. The animists who come to the Lord need to be assured that they are not cast upon their own resources to cope alone.

Referring once more to 2 Cor. 1:22, which speaks of God's Spirit as a deposit, guaranteeing what is to come, the final point is the most pertinent of all for Africans, because they have experienced making deposits as guarantees to agreements. By relating to that custom, the other concepts will open up to them even if they are not initially understood. Such deposits as guarantees are used in the African cultures for purchases, for promised actions, and for binding a marriage arrangement. This is another important bridge point into the culture with the Scriptures.

A similar promise of assurance is found in Ephesians:

> And you also were included in Christ when you heard the word of truth, the gospel of your salvation. Having believed, you were marked by him with a seal, the promised Holy Spirit, who is a deposit guaranteeing our inheritance until the redemption of those who are God's possession—to the praise of his glory.[29]

In addition to the concepts discussed above, there is added here the definite hearing of the word of truth and the response of faith. This indicates clearly that the assurances are intended for believers only. Let this be repeated often and explained carefully to prevent shallow attempts to gain victory. Careful explanation may also prevent discouragement in those seeking the benefits of faith but who have not yet made a personal commitment of faith.

---

[1] 2 Pet. 1:3-4.

[2] Luke 15:10.

[3] 1 Cor. 6:9-10.

[4] 1 Cor. 6:11.

[5] 1 John 3:4-5.

[6] Lev. 4:20.

[7] 2 Chr. 7:14.

[8] Heb. 9:14.

9 John 8:31-32, 36.

10 1 Thess. 1:9-10.

11 Rom. 8:1-2.

12 Heb. 2:14-15.

13 1 Cor. 15:56-57.

14 Heb. 6:18-19.

15 1 John 3:8b.

16 Col. 2:15.

17 Col. 2:10.

18 John 8:36.

19 1 Pet. 3:22.

20 John 14:30.

21 John 10:27-30.

22 2 Thess. 3:3.

23 1 Cor. 1:8-9.

24 Heb. 6:20.

25 Heb. 7:22.

26 2 Cor. 1:21-22.

27 Rom. 8:17.

28 John 14:17-18.

29 Eph. 1:13-14.

13

SCRIPTURAL INSTRUCTIONS TO NEW BELIEVERS

When animists are brought from sorcery to the place of accepting Jesus Christ as Saviour, the chances of their having any accurate Biblical knowledge are slim. Therefore, teaching the new convert must follow on continuously after teaching the same person as a seeker of salvation. Without Bible teaching no one will be able to stand in any culture which is so completely affected with sorcery. There is a strong temptation to take some part of the gospel and run with it to a partial syncretistic faith. This must be countered with scriptural truths.

Four scriptural instructions need to be considered here: withstanding temptation, growing spiritually, doing good works, and praying. A fifth, to study the Word, will be set aside here since new Christians may not have a Bible available, even if it exists in their language. Also, many adults will not be able to read. The serious teaching of the four points mentioned will accomplish the fifth as the Scriptures are read aloud in shared study.

Withstanding Temptation

This section could have been included in the previous section on assurance, because the Scriptures give so much assurance of help and victory in temptation. However, it is included here because there may be additional motivation gained by considering it as a command, while certainly none of the assurances will be lost.

Using sorcery in every part of life, Satan has been able to tempt the animistic people from a very young age. The fear of sorcery disarms them as children, and the practices of sorcery, with their empty promises, overwhelms them as adults. Therefore most of these people are not accustomed to any personal success, because the fatalism supported by sorcery destroys self-confidence. Many of them expect to be overcome because they have been unable to successfully control any part of their destiny. Alternately, they are tempted to try to strike a deal with God and accept a quick fix of partial commitment.

This background is necessary here since the instructions about temptation all speak of (and expect) victory. There must be some psychological adjustments along with the instructions, lest the whole point be misconstrued and discarded with disastrous results.

We must start with Jesus—not with what he said but who he was. We have already referred to the humanity of Jesus while he was here on earth (see Heb. 2:14). He was completely God and yet completely man. The significance of this for the new convert is immediately apparent. We read:

> For we do not have a high priest who is unable to sympathize with our weaknesses, but we have one who has been tempted in every way, just as we are—yet was without sin. Let us then approach the throne of grace with confidence, so that we may receive mercy and find grace to help us in our time of need.[1]

Our high priest is able to intercede for us because he was human, too, and can understand our weakness. He felt what we feel when we are tempted and is able to know what we are facing. This is in extreme contrast to the traditional belief in an absentee God who has departed from all creation. Here is a close personal friend who knows all about us!

Even though Jesus knows all about us and understands our weaknesses, we note that he respects our identity as individuals. Thus, animists cannot expect the high priest of every believer to automatically meet their needs, as an earthly chief might be expected to do. Each believer is to approach the throne of grace with confidence—the believer must be sensitive to needs, take the initiative, and turn to God at the throne of grace. He provides grace and help in the proportions that they are needed, but there is no room for a fatalistic approach which says, "I couldn't help it, it just happened," or "Jesus will help me anyway, it's his responsibility." As a Christian seeks, so shall he find the grace to help in time of need. The humanity of Jesus made this possible. We read earlier in Hebrews: "Because he himself suffered when he was tempted, he is able to help those who are being tempted."[2]

Sorcery perpetuates the fatalistic outlook, but this must not be carried over into the Christian experience. The sorcery-bound people have been deceived to the point that many believe that they are the only ones facing such problems and temptations. This belief leads to despair if it is retained after conversion to Jesus Christ. The Scriptures assure us that this is not true. Paul wrote:

> No temptation has seized you except what is common to man. And God is faithful; he will not let you be tempted beyond what you can bear. But when you are tempted, he will also provide a way out so you can stand up under it.[3]

Not only are animists assured of the universal nature of temptation, they are assured that God is nearby, in fact, he is within each believer, willing that they be able to withstand temptation and doing whatever needs to be done to prevent their defeat. In the midst of the most vicious of all temptations, a Christian can rely on God's power (not his own), and at the same time keep looking for the escape route which God will reveal. When these difficult situations come, the omnipotence of God must be recalled.

Paul prayed that the Ephesians might have the eyes of their hearts enlightened so that (among other things) they might know God's "incomparably great power for us who believe."[4] May the tempted be aware of that power which is ready to help them at all times. This power which is considered the greatest power in the universe, the very same power that resurrected Jesus Christ from death—the very power that gained Jesus the victory over Satan and all his powers!

Later Paul again urges the Ephesians, saying: "Finally, be strong in the Lord and in his mighty power. Put on the full armor of God so that you can take your stand against the devil's schemes."[5] The strength mentioned here is the strength of the Lord, but once again the believer has responsibility. One is to put on and use the armor that has been provided by the grace of God through his plan of salvation. The pieces of armor are truth, righteousness, the gospel, faith, salvation, and the Word of God, followed with prayer. These are provisions supplied by God and are the only things adequate to stand against evil. Throughout Africa the breastplate, the shod feet, and the helmet do not have traditional significance, so even with modern warfare as a substitute, careful explanation is needed to portray the picture of the victorious warrior Paul has in mind.

Also noteworthy is the identification of the enemy—the devil. James gives more light on this, saying: "When tempted, no one should say 'God is tempting me.' For God cannot be tempted by evil, nor does he tempt anyone...."[6] God, then, is completely trustworthy and his power is essential to overcome the devil. This is exactly where the people converted from sorcery to Jesus Christ will have problems. If Satan has surrendered them to salvation in Jesus, surely he will do everything possible to make the conversion a short one. This same identification is made by Peter who declares: "Your enemy the devil prowls around like a roaring lion looking for someone to devour."[7] In Africa lions are a very pertinent point of cultural reference as an enemy. That enemy (the devil) is defeated by each one who accepts Jesus Christ as Saviour, but that enemy will not be completely destroyed until the end times. Therefore, he is able to tempt and to devour—except where the grace of God supplies all that is needed to escape him.

Paul and John give us almost identical statements that are promises to support the Christian. Paul says: "But the Lord is faithful, and he will strengthen and protect you from the evil one."[8] John says: "This is the victory that has overcome the world, even our faith. Who is it that overcomes the world? Only he who believes that Jesus is the Son of God."[9] Protection, victory, and overcoming are the promise of God's Word repeated over and over. The repetition of these themes by the various authors of the New Testament speaks to the importance of these promises. To neglect them is to cause much doubt and strife in the soul of the believer. Once again, the practicality of the Scriptures is seen.

To conclude this section we turn to the book of James. He writes: "Blessed is the man who perseveres under trial, because when he has stood the test, he will receive the crown of life that God has promised to those who love him."[10]

Growing Spiritually

Before turning to the Scriptures and their statements on spiritual growth, let us consider a statement by Dr. George Peters. He says:

> While there is growth and grading among the disciples, there are no graduated disciples. Discipleship is a perpetual school which may lead from one degree to another but does not graduate its scholars.[11]

Growth is a normal part of Christian living and it should not stop before heaven is entered. The animists live close to nature and this concept should be easily accepted and understood.

As the Scriptures are shared and examined with the newly freed people, every attempt should be made to find particularly relevant passages that speak directly to the believers' culture. This has already been mentioned, but it should be a continuing thread that ties God's Word to his people and their life. Searching the Scriptures with this in mind can provide "power points" that penetrate unbelievers' hearts, revealing just how pertinent the Bible is for them. These also become cultural bridges that bring Jesus into the believers' daily life.

From southwestern Congo comes an illustration. Among the Aruund people a chief who is wealthy enough and powerful enough can pay a sorcerer to hide his soul (that is his life) in an animal. This is called *kushil*, and as long as the animal lives, the chief will live. A large animal that lives a long time is best, and the chief must have enough power to effectively prohibit hunting in that area where the animal roams. This is assumed to make it impossible to kill the chief with sorcery powers, since only his personal sorcerer knows where his soul (his life) is hidden.

This well-known belief gives new meaning to Colossians 3:3 where Paul states: "For you have died, and your life is hidden with Christ in God." Through faith in Jesus Christ, any believer can have for certain, on God's Word, what was only uncertainly available to powerful chiefs. Their life is out of the reach of Satan and his sorcery.

When such comparisons are made, it brings the gospel much closer to the culture, and the step of faith does not seem so formidable. Different cultures, and often different tribes, will have different meaningful points of contact. As these are found in increasing numbers, then the Christian faith will appear less and less to be a "foreign" religion.

This should provide a strong incentive for ministering in the language used by the recipient people. Trade languages and international languages, while being helpful in some areas of communication, may prevent injecting the gospel and the Scriptures into a culture. The gospel and the Word of God must be available in the same language used by the people to do their sinning. Only then can the Holy Spirit penetrate as deeply as their sin, and, thus, become as pertinent, as meaningful, and as personally relevant. He, then, can make growth a natural part of Christian faith. A dynamic translation of the Scriptures always speaks best to new Christians, speeding comprehension and thus growth.

Several passages of Scripture admonish the Christian to grow. Peter says: "But grow in the grace and knowledge of our Lord and Saviour Jesus Christ....."[12] As a Christian learns more about Jesus from the Scriptures and from experience, then there is increased capacity to receive grace. That grace is for every need, and as it is accepted, more can be received. Clarke notes that grace is like a seed, and once received it can grow and multiply in the life of a believer. Thus the urgent need for Bible teaching in the most holy sense, and in the most profound dimensions.

Paul was deeply distressed over Christians in Corinth who did not grow. He calls them infants in Christ, and probably they were the same spiritually as when they first believed. Citing worldliness as the cause for their lack of growth, he says: "I gave you milk, not solid food, for you were not ready for it. Indeed, you are still not ready. You are still worldly."[13] Milk is for the new-born babies. These people were acting as babies by not advancing in the grace of God, for they were acting like the unsaved in their dissentions. In his second letter Paul told these people: "And we, who with unveiled faces all reflect the Lord's glory, are being transformed into his likeness with ever-increasing glory."[14] Paul would have all of the Corinthians growing into the likeness of Jesus Christ. We note here that the veil is gone. This may refer to the veil Moses had to wear because of the glory of the Lord, and it may refer to the spiritual veil that prevented the Jews from accepting the Messiah. Either way, the believer is not veiled before Jesus and we are being transformed into his likeness, step by step. This is accomplished only by the grace of God through the work of the indwelling Holy Spirit, and it all comes from the Lord. An open, hungry heart is where he works best.

In teaching this concept of growth to people who have been in sorcery, the goal of that growth must be kept clear. In this instance, it is the likeness of the Lord who is the Holy Spirit. Thus, Paul urges the Ephesians to become mature by attaining the whole measure of Christ. He also tells them (as he told the Corinthians) to quit living like infants. He then admonishes them, saying: "...we will in all things grow up into him who is the head, that is, Christ."[15] Here again is the same goal—a life like that of Jesus. The new convert must not have any people as a pattern for living, nor spiritual goals of his own making. We have only one ultimate example, and that is Jesus Christ. To be like him requires the power and presence of the Holy Spirit filling one's heart, for only the Holy Spirit convicts us of unconfessed sin and reveals the truth of God.

This growth presents us with the same dichotomy mentioned earlier in a different section. God alone has the power to help a person grow into the likeness of Jesus; however, at the same time, there can be no neglecting of the grace and power given to a Christian. The Christian, too, is responsible. Peter says:

> For this very reason, make every effort to add to your faith goodness; and to goodness knowledge; and to knowledge, self control; and to self control, perseverance; and to perseverance, godliness; and to godliness, brotherly kindness; and to brotherly kindness, love.[16]

Because of the promises that we will participate in the divine nature, Peter says we are to make these efforts. God provides the power and the possibility, but each person appropriates that gracious provision by reaching out, seeking to know him better, and desiring above all else to be like him. No person can attain this alone, but neither will God do it for him if he is careless or lazy. Growth includes full participation by God and the believer.

Doing Good Works

The question will be asked, Why are Christians involved in good works? The new Christians will need this issue clarified with the Scriptures, because of the influence of partial involvement by the nominal Christians. Also, in certain parts of Africa the western concept of working for a salary has been totally rejected. Unless spiritual victory is won, good works become a burden to be shunned and the reason for doing them is lost. Likewise, confusion results as to the necessity of good works in relationship to free salvation, and only the Scriptures can give meaning to them.

In Ephesians we find a definite connection between salvation and works. We read: "For we are God's workmanship, created in Christ Jesus to do good works, which God prepared in advance for us to do."[17] Salvation is of God, and he has worked a great work in our hearts—so great that we are a new creation in Jesus. We turned, but he saved; we believed, but he created. This new creature loves God, and loves what God loves, so, therefore, Christians want to do what he wants us to do. His will is to save all who will come to him, and to do all the good through them that people will permit him to do. The believers, then, are created to do those good works which God has arranged for them to do.

This idea is stated by Jesus as he instructed the disciples before sending them out. After giving the list of things they were to do, he told them: "Freely you have received, freely give."[18] This is a commandment, yet what did they receive? They received every good help from Jesus, they were chosen to be saved and used by Jesus, and thus they had received the kingdom of God—freely. Therefore, the command, though firm, was a joyous thing to the disciples, because they were to have a part in the extension of the kingdom of God beyond the twelve. When salvation is genuine, then the commands of God are welcome. John reminds us that God's commands are not burdensome if we have his love in our hearts (see 1 John 5:3). The greatest work of all was on the cross and Jesus did that willingly by the love of God. For those who have the mind of Christ, there can only be joy connected with good works. The people who were bound by sorcery have seen very lit-

164

tle of this kind of love and this kind of good works. They need the illumination of the Holy Spirit upon the Scriptures at this point; then they will know what to expect and what is expected of them.

God expects several things in our good works. Among these are our witness, our help to others, our gifts, and our example. The first is illustrated by Jesus when he cast the demons from a man; he refused to let the man follow him. Instead he said: "Return home and tell how much God has done for you."[19] Jesus expected that man to witness to what he had experienced. He was to witness in his own family where he would be most effective. Before he ascended, Jesus also told the disciples that they were to be his witnesses. This was no small thing, because the word "witness" actually refers to someone who gives testimony to the truth even at the expense of their life.

This is serious business (as the cross indicates), but it is all joy if there is true faith and a new person in Jesus Christ. In addition, God expects a Christian to help others in their needs, both spiritually and physically. John indicates that we have a special responsibility to fellow believers. He says: "We ought, therefore, to show hospitality to such men (workers of the church) so that we may work together for the truth."[20] Those who serve the Lord are not only worthy of help, they are also worthy of being brothers in a united effort for that work. The writer of Hebrews also urges this as a considered and planned effort. We note: "And let us consider how we may spur one another on toward love and good deeds."[21] Christians are to go out of their way to encourage one another in these things, and not sit back to wait for someone else to do what needs to be done. It is significant that love in this verse precedes good works—it always does in the soul of an obedient Christian.

Next, God expects our gifts. He had a definite plan for the tithe and this was the base of all giving in the Law (see Num. 18:26 ff.). Since Jesus came to fulfill the Law and not to destroy it, we can assume that the tithe is the current base as well. Speaking to nominal followers of God, Jesus called them hypocrites, because they gave their tithe but neglected the more important spiritual matters of the heart. However, Jesus supported tithing, saying: "You should have practiced the latter, without neglecting the former."[22]

The spirit of giving is very important—it should come from a heart full of God's love. Such giving is always seen and rewarded by God himself. Jesus declared:

> Give and it will be given to you. A good measure, pressed down, shaken together and running over, will be poured into your lap. For with the measure you use, it will be measured to you.[23]

Such precise generosity will be strange to new Christians who have been tied to sorcery. Their life has been lived with a plan to give in order to get back, or to give in order to influence someone in their favor—in other words, bribery. The authority of God's Word, which is over all people, together with the loving revelations of the Holy Spirit, can bring understanding and growth.

God has been, and expects to be, very generous to his own children, and he expects them to be generous in all good works. This spirit of giving is not forced upon us, even as salvation was not a matter of coercion. Paul explains: "Each man should give what he has decided in his heart to give, not reluctantly or under compulsion, for God loves a cheerful giver."[24] God wants the giving of these gifts to be his extension in the world—he has no other means of giving, so he promises to supply and resupply believers who are generous so his will may be accomplished in love.

Our last consideration of the things God expects in our good works is our example. Peter urges believers, saying: "Live such good lives among the pagans that, though they accuse you of doing wrong, they may see your good deeds and glorify God on the day he visits us."[25] The good deeds done among the animistic people will have this same effect, if they come from a full heart blessed of God. The deeds, of course, each have their own purpose, but in addition to that purpose there is the benefit which observers gain. Though unbelievers ridicule and make accusations against these things, in the end they, too, will see the glory of God in them. Paul writes to Titus, saying: "In everything set them an example by doing what is good."[26] Good works, carried out in the manner explained to us in the Scriptures, are a powerful example that can be a tool in reaching others for Christ.

There are so many truths related to the good works of believers that it may appear to be an impossible, overwhelming task to fulfill all of them. Two considerations help the Christian over this possible despair. First, Jesus said: "Remain in me, and I will remain in you. No branch can bear fruit by itself; it must remain in the vine. Neither can you bear fruit unless you remain in me."[27] He knows that each Christian can not do good works on his own. Yet if we continue in our faith and do not turn aside, he will continue to be with us and nurture us. We can all be fruitful because of him.

Second, we are part of the body of Christ, his church. Paul tells about the variety of spiritual gifts which are given to different members of the church: "There are different kinds of gifts but the same spirit. There are different kinds of service, but the same Lord." These gifts are for different kinds of work that make up the whole ministry. After listing the variety of gifts, Paul adds: "All these are the work of one and the same Spirit, and he gives them to each man, just as he determines."[28] These passages, along with other references to the work of the body, should be thoroughly studied by the new Christians, so they can see themselves as a part of the ongoing church and not as an individual suddenly isolated from others. They have a long line of ancestors in Christ Jesus, going back all the way to the Biblical times. The good works performed by the new converts will help to solidify their position in the church as the members are mutually beneficial.

We must continually count on the Holy Scriptures to instruct and to inspire the new Christian who turns from sorcery. While the newly created Christian has the love of God in his heart as a source for all good works, there are many indications in the Scriptures that this is not necessarily an automatic process. It requires teaching and growing and telling. Referring to the man from whom Jesus removed the demons, we noted that at first he did not naturally want to do what Jesus wanted him to do. Jesus had to tell him what to do and then he was obedient. Paul writes: "I want you to stress these things, so that those who have trusted in God may be careful to devote themselves to doing what is good."[29] Here is an admonition that must bring teaching the Scriptures into the essential center of the ministry to the sorcery-bound people. If good works are the desired end result, we, too, must stress many scriptural truths.

Instructions for Prayer

The first prayer for the person in bondage is a prayer of confession, and the second is a prayer for mercy. These are followed by prayers of faith, and then by an endless series of prayers. There is much prayer to idols among animists, as well as prayer to God. However, these are prayers offered, and not prayers answered. There is no communion with the object of their petition, no answer is expected, and the specific benefit prayed for is a loosely held hope. Against this background of prayer experience, the person freed from sorcery must immediately become involved in a scriptural prayer life. This will be a lifeline for him as he turns from his past and anticipates the future.

The Scriptures teach many things about prayer, but we will consider only the basic essentials for the new believer and not all the ramifications of a mature ministry of prayer. These are: learning to pray regularly, learning to praise and give thanks, learning to seek guidance, and learning to maintain victory.

Praying regularly—Jesus used a parable to teach his disciples that they should be persistent in prayer and never give up (see Luke 18:1-8). This parable tells of a widow who needed justice from an evil judge. Even though he did not care about her or anyone else, he gave her justice because of her persistence. Jesus concludes:

> Listen to what the unjust judge says. And will not God bring about justice for his chosen ones who cry to him day and night? Will he keep putting them off? I tell you he will see that they get justice and quickly.[30]

This gives us confidence to pray regularly and persistently, trusting God to answer. We note here, however, that all prayer is to be according to his will or the persistence is futile (see 1 John 5:14).

Paul also declares: "Be joyful always; pray continually; give thanks in all circumstances, for this is God's will for you in Christ Jesus."[31] The theme of this passage is the continuing nature of the heart of the believer. By the grace which God gives us, the joy, the prayers, and the thanks never stop flowing. There are differences in these and the prayers offered to idols or in sorcery practices. The joy, the prayers, and the thanksgiving are not restricted to a place or time, and also, these flow from a full heart, not a desperate heart. Therefore, each new Christian must be taught how to begin in this unceasing prayer and fellowship with his God. These prayers are to be expressed in Jesus' name (see John 14:13) and according to the will of God. This fellowship gives hope for the new Christian as he begins to pray.

Praising God and giving thanks—Learning to praise and give thanks may be difficult for an animist. Praise words are used for chiefs and also for idols, but the content does not mean the same in those contexts as it does for the Christian. While praise words in the traditional religion may be quite hollow or even a deceptive device used to hide true feelings, the Christian praises God sincerely from a full, overflowing heart. Thanksgiving is not an obligation, but rather a showing forth of gratitude for blessings that are beyond comprehension. This should be an automatic and spontaneous emotion with the believer; but without learning it from the Scriptures it may be missed, or at least misdirected. Jesus healed ten lepers, but only one returned to give thanks. Jesus said: "Were not all ten cleansed? Where are the other nine? Was no one found to return and give praise to God except this foreigner?"[32] This one pleased Jesus—the one with genuine faith. We do not know what happened to the other nine, but certainly they had not learned to be thankful or to praise. When Jesus taught the twelve disciples to pray, he included first the praise of God the Father (see Luke 11:2).

Praise appears most often in the Psalms, and some of them are only for praising. This should be the textbook for teaching new Christians to praise, for many of the expressions indicate a full and blessed heart. The Psalmist exclaims:

My heart is steadfast, O God;
I will sing and make music with all my soul.
Awake, harp and lyre!
I will awaken the dawn.
I will praise you, O LORD, among the nations;
I will sing of you among the peoples.[33]

If anyone has found salvation through the gospel of Jesus Christ, this song of praise must be a great teacher in the art of thanksgiving.

Seeking guidance—Learning to seek guidance through prayer follows the praise and thanksgiving. What would he have me to do? Where is my place in the body of Christ? These are legitimate questions that must be considered prayerfully in light of the Scriptures. We are assured that God does the arranging of the body of Christ, the Church, for we read: "But in fact God has arranged the parts of the body, every one of them, just as he wanted them to be."[34] Here the new convert discovers for a certainty that it is God's will for each Christian to be in the right place in the church. That place should be sought with the diligence mentioned earlier. One of the most encouraging passages for anyone seeking God's will is found in the Psalms.

I will instruct you and teach you in the way you should go;
I will counsel you and watch over you.[35]

With this assurance a new convert should be able to pray on with certainty and patience, waiting on the Lord.

In the book of Acts, at the beginning of the Church, the early Christians prayed for guidance and God heard and answered prayer. Two illustrations encourage any seeker today. First, when the disciples had to choose a replacement for Judas, the choice was made by a group of about 120 people who were joined together constantly in prayer (see Acts 1:14). Peter referred to the Scriptures for instructions to make the choice (see v. 16) and specific prayer followed that. They prayed: "Lord you know everyone's heart. Show us which of these two you have chosen to take over this apostolic ministry, which Judas left to go where he belongs."[36] The lot then fell to Matthias—a decision based on the continuing prayer and guidance of the Word of God. This praying for guidance must replace the divining found in the traditional religions. Some have suggested the Scriptures as a replacement for such practices, but surely they must be closely coupled to prayer. The Scriptures cannot stand alone, lest they be misused as a form of magic.

The second illustration is the call of Barnabas and Paul. This call was definite and understood by all. It was the work of the Holy Spirit among people who were gathered together worshiping the Lord and fasting. These prayerful activities provided an atmosphere where they were sensitive to the guidance of the Holy Spirit, and they displayed a willingness to be led by him. Any guidance involves obedience, so we read: "So after they had fasted and prayed, they placed their hands on them and sent them off."[37] Guidance through prayer has countless illustrations, but the important thing is to be convinced by the Word that it works and is a part of God's plan.

Maintaining victory—Learning to maintain victory through prayer can give a new Christian the confidence to persevere in faith. In the section above on assurance, we mentioned that Jesus Christ our Lord intercedes for us. This needs to be taught thoroughly, because there is no true hope for victory without his intercession, and with it there is every hope. Peter had much difficulty with Satan. He was often tempted and he failed the test several times. But Jesus cared, as attested to in this Scripture: "Simon, Simon, Satan has asked to sift you as wheat.But I have prayed for you, Simon, that your faith may not fail. And when you have turned back, strengthen your brothers."[38] This same Jesus cares for each Christian in the same way. The prayers offered up in his name are presented to the throne of God by him. How encouraging to read: "Therefore he is able to save completely those who come to God through him because he always lives to intercede for them."[39] At the same time we read: "In the same way, the Spirit helps us in our weakness. We do not know what we ought to pray, but the Spirit himself intercedes for us with groans that words cannot express."[40]

Jesus warned the disciples about their weakness and the power of prayer. He told them in the Garden of Gethsemane: "Watch and pray so that you will not fall into temptation. The spirit is willing but the body is weak."[41] He realized that their intentions were good but that they were powerless to follow through. Through prayer they would be able to maintain the victory which he later gave them, and through prayer they could overcome temptation.

The new Christians who remain in their culture and in their families may be very lonely. Old friends, spirits, deceased ancestors who were thought to be close, are suddenly gone. There may be no other person near who understands their step of faith, and they will need to see prayer as a communion, or a fellowship, with Jesus Christ their Lord. To learn to share with him and to recognize his presence is a special function of prayer that can be a great comfort. The Aruund people of Congo have a very meaningful expression, *mu umwing*. Literally it means "in one," but it expresses a very intimate relationship of "oneness." Jesus calls us to remain in him (see John 15:1-17), and this expression captures this meaning—another cultural link.

And how can a Christian continue if sin enters his life? The Scriptures also deal with this, and they give hope even to the one who has missed the mark. Speaking to Christians, John says:

> If we claim to be without sin, we deceive ourselves and the truth is not in us. If we confess our sins, he is faithful and just and will forgive us our sins and purify us from all unrighteousness.[42]

Confession, forgiveness, and cleansing restore the truly penitent one to faith and a vital relationship with Jesus Christ. Teaching these truths can prevent defeat and despair which so easily overwhelm new Christians.

To summarize thus far, these are the basics of a ministry to the sorcery-bound people. They are based on the Scriptures so the Word of God (and not the word of man) can speak to their problems and their victories. This chapter gives the upward thrust of the Scriptures, but these are only the beginning. As these are taught carefully, at a speed which assures comprehension, more illustrations and verses will come to light to expand this beginning. The urgent necessity is to bring the believers from their point of turning, all the way into a faith established in the Scriptures. Only this will give an unshakable base for faith that will endure to the end. There must be teaching prior to any decision and there must be teaching for growth following that initial decision. The Scriptures are pertinent and practical at every stage of salvation, and they alone through the Holy Spirit are the adequate source for spiritual information.

---

1 Heb. 4:15-16.

2 Heb. 2:18.

3 1 Cor. 10:13.

4 Eph. 1:18-19.

5 Eph. 6:10-11.

6 Jas. 1:13.

7 1 Pet. 5:8.

8 2 Thess. 3:3.

9 1 John 5:4-5.

10 Jas. 1:12.

11 George W. Peters, *A Biblical Theology of Missions* (Chicago: Moody Press, 1972), p. 189.

12 2 Pet. 3:18.

13 1 Cor. 3:2-3.

14 2 Cor. 3:18.

15 Eph. 4:15.

16 2 Pet. 1:5-7.

17 Eph. 2:10.

18 Matt. 10:8.

19 Luke 8:39.

20 3 John 8.

21 Heb. 10:24.

22 Matt. 23:23.

23 Luke 6:38.

24 2 Cor. 9:7.

25 1 Pet. 2:12.

26 Titus 2:7.

27 John 15:4.

28 1 Cor. 12:4-5, 11.

29 Titus 3:8.

30 Luke 18:6-8.

31 1 Thess. 5:16-18.

32 Luke 17:17.

33 Ps. 108:1-3.

34 1 Cor. 12:18.

35 Ps. 32:8.

36 Acts 1:24-25.

37 Acts 13:3.

38 Luke 22:31.

39 Heb. 7:25.

40 Rom. 8:26.

41 Matt. 26:41.

42 1 John 1:8-9.

14

SCRIPTURAL GOALS
IN MATURITY

The Holy Spirit has been mentioned often throughout the material presented in this proposed ministry. However, the work of the Holy Spirit is so uniquely important that it will be considered separately here to get some important considerations in proper perspective. The active ingredient of power in the struggle with sorcery is God, the Holy Spirit; therefore, his presence is indispensable.

Tippett speaks of a specific consummation of the Christian experience among some of the Pacific islanders:

> The Wesleyans' interpretation was to see these consummation experiences as a second work of grace, what Paul called <u>deuteran charin</u> (second grace), and immediately after conversion they strove for the sanctifying experience. But whatever name we give it, and whatever way we explain it, we cannot escape two clear facts: the experience was real and widespread; and it had a remarkable after-effect on the lives it touched.[1]

Dr. Robert E. Coleman, Director of the School of World Mission and Evangelism at Trinity Evangelical Divinity School, notes in his book on evangelism that the disciples required a special enduement of power to face the task before them:

> This meant that the disciples through confession of their deep seated pride and enmity in utter surrender of

themselves to Christ had to come by faith into a new and refining experience of the Spirit's infilling.[2]

These men are speaking of the pentecostal experience which came in Acts, chapter two, and the same experience which men received centuries later in Southern Polynesia. The results of the first can be followed all through the book of Acts (and the remainder of the New Testament) and the results of the latter are in the records of the mission churches. Victorious Christians who are fruitful are the natural result of Pentecost.

Bishop Ngoi Wakadilo, Rev. Nshid Sampas, and Dr. Katenga Mbuya have all reported separately that the dynamic of the Holy Spirit is needed to minister to the sorcery-bound people of Africa. Without this, all three despair of any victory over the sorcery problem. With this in mind, we turn to the Scriptures to find the basis for this experience. We will consider here the Scriptures relating to the infilling of the Holy Spirit, the work of the Holy Spirit, and the experience of yielding to the Holy Spirit. These overlap, but each has a special emphasis.

The Infilling of the Holy Spirit

Jesus told his disciples that they had an enormous task before them. It certainly was too much for their experience up to the time of the crucifixion. They knew Jesus to be the Messiah, they had believed in him and been discipled by him, but they were not ready to face the world as witnesses to him. This is indicated by the fearful group hiding behind locked doors on the day of the resurrection. After teaching them more truths following his resurrection, Jesus commanded them:

> Do not leave Jerusalem, but wait for the gift my Father promised which you have heard me speak about. For John baptized with water, but in a few days you will be baptized with the Holy Spirit.[3]

This was not a suggestion but a command from Jesus. Likewise, Paul instructed the Ephesians, saying: "Be filled with the Spirit."[4] (Literally, be continually being filled.) He also told these same people: "...to know this love that surpasses knowledge—that you may

178

be filled to the measure of all the fullness of God."⁵ He also prayed
that they might be strengthened by the power of the Holy Spirit in
their inner being (see Eph. 3:16). To the Romans he said: "May the
God of hope fill you with all joy and peace as you trust in him, so
that you may overflow with hope by the power of the Holy
Spirit."⁶

These Scriptures all indicate that the experience of the infilling of the Holy Spirit is not only possible but it is an integral part
of the Christian experience. Since these statements were made to
Christians, it is reasonable to assume that there is a distinct experience of filling that is separate from the initial salvation which
Christ accomplishes in the repentant sinner's heart. The Holy
Spirit is sent by Christ himself (see John 15:26), and his work in
the believer is to glorify Christ (see v. 14), to guide him into all
truth, and to give power to his life. Paul tells us: "Now the Lord
is the Spirit"⁷ and this reveals that the Holy Spirit is the third person of the Holy Trinity, yet one with God. Christ told his disciples:
"And surely I will be with you always, to the very end of the age."⁸
This promise is kept in the form of the Holy Spirit; so in a very
special sense the indwelling Holy Spirit is the indwelling Christ,
who is God himself. These things are all extremely important to
the person who is reaching toward growth and a mature experience that will provide the power for an effective life of victory that
bears much fruit for the Kingdom of God.

The Power of the Holy Spirit

It is not necessary to go into detail about the power that was
manifested in the book of Acts. We need only mention that that
was the power which motivated people and accomplished mighty
things in the early church. Of more importance here is the effect
of that power on the believer as indicated by the Scriptures.

The power of the Spirit to overcome sin in the believer's life is
mentioned by Paul. He says: "So I say, live by the Spirit, and you
will not gratify the desires of the sinful nature."⁹ For all sinners, the
desire of their life has been to satisfy the basic selfish desires and
appetites, so power is needed to overcome that natural practice
of natural desire. According to God's Word, Christians can live a
holy life through the power of the Holy Spirit.

Another work of that power is to produce qualities of life that are good and Christ-like. We read: "But the fruit of the Spirit is love, joy, peace, patience, kindness, goodness, faithfulness, gentleness and self control."[10] These qualities are those which come out from the heart of man, and they must be the result of a change in the inner self, in fact, a new heart. Mankind is naturally sinful, doing evil things (see Gal. 5:19-20), so the Holy Spirit must change the nature of a person in order to change the fruit of the new life. To do this he must be invited to infill or indwell the believer as surrender is made completely to God's will. This may be a distinct experience at any point in the growth process, following the experience of salvation. Usually there is spiritual growth prior to this infilling and continuing growth following a definite experience of infilling. A sincerely seeking soul can trust the Holy Spirit to direct and accomplish this experience. Animists who find the Living Christ as their Saviour will understand the meaning of the story Jesus told about the man who had an evil spirit cast out of him (see Luke 11:24-26).

The power of the Holy Spirit's intercession is the center of assurance for believers. As a new Christian faces disappointment, doubt, and temptation of all kinds, that person can pray and have help even with the content of the prayer. Paul writes:

> We do not know what we ought to pray, but the Spirit himself intercedes for us with groans that words cannot express...the Spirit intercedes for the saints in accordance with God's will.[11]

The power and presence of the Holy Spirit sanctifies the believer, for we read: "But you were washed, you were sanctified, you were justified in the name of the Lord Jesus Christ and by the Spirit of our God."[12] Paul declared that his ministry was to the Gentiles, and he also said: "...so that the Gentiles might become an offering acceptable to God, sanctified by the Holy Spirit."[13] Sanctification includes the concepts of setting aside a life for God's use, and of purifying a life for holy living. The animists who have great regard for sanctified objects, places, and leaders will also grasp the significance of this work of the Holy Spirit. The guide to the application of this experience in the life of each believer must always be the Scriptures, in order to prevent a syncretistic mixture of beliefs.

These glimpses of the power of the Holy Spirit show how essential is his presence among the sorcery-bound people. This is precisely the life and the ministry that is needed to free people from sorcery and to bring them to victory.

Yielding to the Holy Spirit

When a person is converted and is born again by faith in Jesus Christ, that new believer receives the Holy Spirit. The Scripture says:

> You, however, are controlled not by the sinful nature but by the Spirit, if the Spirit of God lives in you. And if anyone does not have the Spirit of Christ, he does not belong to Christ.[14]

In order to be complete, however, the Christian's goal must be a full and complete yielding to the will of God—a willingness for one's will to be controlled by the Holy Spirit. We have already mentioned about the fullness and overflowing (see Rom. 15:13).

Even after a complete yielding there is still the growing to be like him (see Eph. 4:13), as we mature into the fullness of Christ. Paul tells the Philippians: "...for it is God who works in you to will and to act according to his good purpose."[15]

Our loving God is working, and we must be yielding continually in order to reach the correct end result. Too many new Christians have slipped into error or slipped back into sorcery and sin when the Holy Spirit's ministry has been minimized or neglected. Jesus stated the goal clearly in the midst of the Sermon on the Mount: "Be perfect, therefore, as your heavenly Father is perfect."[16] Fortunately, we have not been left on our own to seek that perfection which is not so much a perfect performance (because Jesus alone was perfect in that sense) as a perfect intent to be yielded to God's perfect will. This yielding of self to God increases the capacity for filling the soul with the Holy Spirit, and thus spiritual growth is experienced.

The Scriptures are definite about the Holy Spirit's power and his availability. There is a general desire to obtain the numerous benefits of the Holy Spirit. However, the stumbling block to the fullness of the Spirit may lie not in the receiving but in the yielding.

The Greatest Commandment

Jesus did not say that to be filled with the Holy Spirit was the greatest commandment. The Scriptures read:

> "The most important one," answered Jesus, "is this: 'Hear, O Israel, the Lord our God, the Lord is one. Love the Lord your God with all your heart and with all your soul and with all your mind and with all your strength.' The second is this: 'Love your neighbor as yourself.' There is no commandment greater than these."[17]

If we are to love that much, then there is no place for selfish love or love of material things. The greatest commandment commands us to be willing to be cleansed from all unrighteousness (see 1 John 1:9) and to walk with him in that supreme kind of love. Those who seek the Holy Spirit in complete fullness will find him when all selfish love is yielded and all cleansing is accepted from him. He can then fill that emptied, cleansed soul and bring his gifts into that life for ministry within the body of Christ. Likewise, the Holy Spirit will bear his fruit in each willing life. His love will free them to love as indicated in the greatest commandment. Such spiritual maturity is the goal for this ministry among the sorcery-bound people.

---

1 Tippett, *Polynesia*, p. 84.

2 Robert E. Coleman, *The Master Plan of Evangelism* (Old Tappan: Fleming H. Revell Co., 1963), p. 69.

3 Acts 1:4-5.

4 Eph. 5:18.

5 Eph. 3:19.

6 Rom. 15:13.

7 2 Cor. 3:17.

8 Matt. 28:20.

9 Gal. 5:16.

10 Gal. 5:22-23.

11 Rom. 8:26.

12 1 Cor. 6:11.

13 Rom. 15:16.

14 Rom. 8:9.

15 Phil. 2:13.

16 Matt. 5:48.

17 Mark 12:29-31.

PART III

APPLICATION
OF THE MINISTRY TO
SORCERY-BOUND PEOPLE

15

PREPARING
TO MINISTER

The Church will probably be the base for the outreach of the ministry to sorcery-bound people. There exist at the present time various mission churches that carry on extensive work in the cities, as well as in the bush areas. In recent years younger churches have begun work which is concentrated in one area.

Because of the ministry of these many churches, there are those who have found victory in Jesus Christ and their lives witness to Christian commitment. According to African church leaders, however, few of the members are truly committed Christians, while the vast majority are only nominal followers of the Church. Therefore, leadership for a ministry to the sorcery-bound will have to come from the former group. However, the first outreach of this ministry may be to the second group (the nominal Christians) who have had varying amounts of exposure to the Christian message.

In order for the ministry to be effective, the actual situation in which the receptor people exist must be ascertained. Any effort will be non-productive if the ministers to the people do not comprehend the particular problems of those being ministered to. In Congo, for example, this has all too often been the situation. Likewise, leadership that has no spiritual victory within its own ranks will not be able to minister effectively to sorcery-bound people. Therefore, the preparation phase must precede any ministry. This includes three steps: Identifying the victorious Christians, measuring the readiness of the people, and analyzing the local conditions.

Identifying the Victorious Christians

Victorious Christians can be found anywhere. They may already be involved in a work for the Lord or they may be members of a village church. Both of these types of Christians may have training or they may be barely able to read the Bible. They may be men or women, young or old. Whatever their circumstances, they have one thing in common—they have a faith in Jesus Christ and a victory over sorcery and other sins, by the power of the Holy Spirit. These people are not numerous; however, they must be identified because they will form the beginning of any ministry to the sorcery-bound people. These victorious Christians may be considered "innovators."

Identifying these people is an essential beginning, because all of the ministry that follows will depend on them. Their number is not important—one person is enough for a start. However, if not even one such person is found in a particular area, then a victorious, Spirit-filled missionary, who has a sensitive grasp of the culture and language, could be the one who will make such a beginning. In many areas there is great freedom for cross-cultural ministry.

When more than one Spirit-filled Christian is located for ministry, then they should be united in a prayer group—regardless of differences in training or background. In these groups prayerful consideration must be given to help everyone understand the purpose and the method of the work. In fact, regardless of their previous training, these trainees should be given intensive teaching of the Scriptures as outlined in previous chapters. They must see the ministry from a Biblical perspective and understand just how the ministry will progress. Thus the taught ones become the teachers.

Measuring Readiness to Receive Ministry

This step is more precise than the first one. It is this step that will indicate which field is ripe for harvest; that is, where the Holy Spirit is working and preparing hearts to receive his Word. Three groups of people must be measured to determine this: the pastors (or church leaders where there is no ordained ministry), the laity, and the youth.

The pastors—The first step is the development of questionnaires. Questionnaire 1 (see appendix) is designed as an example for pastors or leaders to determine their knowledge of their traditional religion of animism. This questionnaire can be changed to meet the needs of any group. Pastors who are raised in urban settings have different traditional beliefs than those raised in villages, and often neither group knows of this difference. This can also happen when pastors move from one area to another without studying the beliefs of the new congregation. Earlier we stressed the general similarities of animistic religion in various places, but in this ministry the details of the local needs must be understood. It is possible for leaders to misunderstand the sorcery problems of the people in a certain area, especially if they have been away attending school for a number of years. It is also possible for leaders to be involved in sorcery, or more commonly, to be ineffective because of fear of sorcery. This questionnaire will help to measure their actual awareness of the problem of sorcery.

Further measurement is possible with Questionnaire 2 (see appendix). This questionnaire includes a subjective series of questions to help clarify the Christian experience and beliefs of the leaders. The questions vary from specific to general. Cross-examination type questions help to indicate the degree of accuracy of the answers. These questionnaires should be administered at a conference or some such meeting where the leaders can fill in the answers without discussing them. Instructions should be clearly given to indicate that individual answers are required. At the same time confidentiality (no names are used) must be assured in order to obtain honest answers. There are no negative questions which can be confused with western answers of yes and no, because these are easily misunderstood cross-culturally. It may be advisable to read each question aloud to the group as they fill out the questionnaire.

Tabulation of these questionnaire responses will give an indication of the depth of Christian faith and the amount of understanding of the sorcery problem. Along with the structured questions it is advisable to give opportunity for anyone to express themselves about the problem of sorcery. Pastors are also accustomed to sharing their convictions; so in this way much can be learned about each person.

The laity—The next step is to evaluate the laity in order to locate capable leadership and to assess their needs. Questionnaire

2 is helpful for this purpose. If the lay people are accustomed to thinking through their faith, they will also provide helpful information by using Questionnaire 1.

If some folks are illiterate, others will need to read the questions for them and then mark the answers. If time is an important factor (it seldom is), then a shift to Questionnaire 3 will help, since it is much shorter and can be administered more quickly by a trained interviewer. During a seminar, time should also be provided for free discussion of the sorcery problems. Regardless of how these discussions are conducted, it is important for the leaders of this ministry to listen with prayerful consideration to all that is said, because this will give an indication of what the Holy Spirit is doing in preparation for the coming ministry. The intensity of interest, the depth of perception, and the amount of desire to be free from sorcery are all important.

Preliminary seminars may also be held for homogeneous groups, such as women's meetings in churches. Some topics are not permitted to be discussed when members of the opposite sex are present. At other times there may be much more diversity in the discussions if a mixture of men, women, and youth are present. A series of meetings which will utilize each method will give the best results.

Seminar follow-up is essential. After the discussions have stimulated thinking and opinions, the people will begin to have deeper thoughts and increased insights. In the days which immediately follow the seminar, individuals may ask questions which may be more revealing because they are asked without the pressures of the group or an unexpected questionnaire. From these contacts, Spirit-filled, victorious persons who can share this ministry may be found.

Along with the expressions of their own beliefs and circumstances, one must identify the laity's level of understanding of the Biblical hope. During discussions and interviews one must take note of any correct Biblical concepts, as well as the misinformation which may exist in the local group. This will provide clues as to where the ministry will begin, how fast it can progress, as well as revealing cultural contact points.

When measuring pastors or laity, one must be sensitive to suggestions from each group. The local variations are important to the local people, and an effective ministry will take all these factors

190

into consideration.

The youth—It is known that youth by nature are curious, and this curiosity can be put to good use by measuring their understanding of sorcery and the Bible. It was mentioned earlier that the modern youth are seeking an understanding of sorcery-related activities. They often have a very superficial comprehension of the Bible unless they have been discipled. Questionnaire 4 has been designed with youth in mind, so that those who minister to them will have some grasp of their present level of understanding.

The administration of the questionnaire would ideally take place in a youth meeting, where careful instructions could be given without discussing the questions or answers. Instructions are not given on the questionnaire because of cross-cultural differences in asking and answering questions. In the case of youth, homogeneous groups are recommended. There will be less friction within groups who are all of similar school level.

Once again, discussion can provide many insights. Notes, or even tapes, should be kept of these exchanges of opinions for later comparison with the questionnaires. It is possible, however, that tape recorders will cause too much artificial stimuli. Therefore, mental notes taken by leaders may be more accurate, since they allow for complete freedom in the group.

The measurement of the readiness of the people to receive a ministry to sorcery can provide important clues, and evaluation is time well spent. Dr. James Engel, communications professor at Wheaton College graduate school, states:

> Research, along with intuition and experience, is an indispensable aspect of the arsenal of the Christian communicator. It is a necessity in a rapidly changing world because there is no other accurate way to find the pulse of the audience.... Research does not short-circuit the work of the Holy Spirit but rather provides an essential avenue through which He can lead.[1]

Analysis of the Setting for the Ministry

The final step in preparing for the ministry to the sorcery-bound people is to analyze the setting in which it will occur. This combines the many facets of the existing situation in which the people live, as well as all the information collected in the various research measurements for interpretation. The goal of this analysis is to find a group or groups where the Holy Spirit is actively preparing for such a ministry. Tippett tells us that there are many scriptural references which refer to timely harvests. He states:

> ...for the present day missionary, they must signify that all fields do not come ripe for harvest at the same time. This involves us in the task of recognizing a ripe field and attending to the ingathering, even though it mean deployment of personnel from unripe areas.[2]

When a certain field (or group) is prepared by the Holy Spirit, a ministry for the sorcery-bound people should begin among them. In Congo, for example, more than one hundred people turned up for a seminar on sorcery for which forty invitations had been sent. Such a response indicated that people were eager to have guidance and help to find a way out of their endless bondage to sorcery.

Tabulation will indicate areas where the people are most responsive, whether in cities or rural areas. Likewise, when the youth analysis is compared with the analysis of the laity, one can determine to whom and where the ministry will be aimed. Biblical opinions held by the people will be important, for this will help to guide teachers to the points that need extra emphasis or correction.

The tabulation results will be considered in light of the impressions gained from conversations with individuals, the discussions held at the various meetings, and the intuition of the leaders. All of these must be prayerfully considered lest there be a rushing off to start ministering in some ineffective manner. The non-numerical considerations relate to the careful observation of the problems facing people. For example, one Congolese leader indicated that the uncertainty of war caused an increase in sorcery practices. Another leader, however, pointed out that war in one city had turned people to the Church and to renewed faith. Even though these reports come from people who are separated from each other by hundreds of miles, these are the types of incidents which must be a part of the evaluation.

Another special condition that may affect the readiness for

ministry is displacement due to war or famine. Refugees are often more open to the introduction of a new ministry; however, if there is bitterness toward a particular group of people, which includes the leaders of this ministry, then the door may be temporarily closed to the gospel that will set them free. The important thing to note here is that every piece of information gathered from the various groups must be considered. God gives gifts, blessings, and promises to all who turn to him, but he expects us to use all the tools he has provided for developing an effective ministry. The questionnaires and related information from the people can help us work together with the Holy Spirit.

There is much work to be done by men of God; however, Hesselgrave reminds us:

> All the same, the ultimate factor in the receptivity of a people will be whether or not the Holy Spirit of God has been allowed to prepare the hearts of respondent peoples.[3]

---

[1] James Engel, *How Can I Get Them to Listen?* (Grand Rapids: Zondervan Publishing House, 1977), p. 23.

[2] Tippett, *Polynesia*, p. 209.

[3] Hesselgrave, *Communicating Christ Cross-Culturally*, p.270.

16

SPECIFIC
PROCEDURES
FOR PRESENTATION

The application of this ministry to the sorcery-bound people, as developed in previous chapters, should follow the above preparations, which should then insure the most profitable use of the resources available. While making these preparations before ministering is ideal, a word of warning is needed before proceeding. In the first place, ministries or programs rarely follow a pre-planned outline because there are too many unforeseen variables. In the second place, over-preparation may also result in no actual work being accomplished. Therefore, if delays occur in preparation, this ministry to the sorcery-bound people should proceed wherever even one victorious Christian is discovered. Such leaders should be trained while the preparations for locating ripe fields are being pursued. As opportunities in such ripe fields are discovered, and receptive people will listen to the Word, then teaching, preaching, and witnessing must proceed immediately.

Six specific procedures are listed here. They are not exhaustive proposals, but suggestions that will hopefully give guidance to anyone who proposes to carry out such a ministry.

1. Teach the Scriptures as outlined in Part II, first to the victorious leaders and then to those in the ripe fields. As mentioned earlier, the order of presentation is important because of the progression of the decision making process. The gospel is the good news that brings salvation, but when ministering to the sorcery-bound people, the gospel will be easily misunderstood without ade-

quate scriptural teaching. If each person knows the Word of God well, he can then relate to God through the Holy Spirit, instead of relating to the evangelist or teacher.

Keeping the steps separate in the minds of the seekers requires patient persistence and a willingness on the part of the teacher to proceed only as each point is understood. In the parable of the sower only one out of four seeds grew to maturity and produced fruit. This one not only <u>heard</u> the Word, but he also <u>understood</u> it (see Matthew 13). The victorious Christian who opens the Scriptures to sorcery-bound people is not expected to change anyone; God does that. However, the teacher is responsible for sowing the Word in such a way that it can be understood and inspire growth into maturity.

2. Encourage memorization of the Scriptures. Whether or not the seekers have the Bible available to them in an understandable language, they must still have the portions taught in their own "heart" language. To repeat, the Scriptures must be presented in the same language which is used for sinning. In order to strike at the root of the problem in the soul, the message must agree linguistically with the thought patterns of the individual that control the spiritual part of their life. This is not only true for cross-cultural communication by the missionary, but for the pastor or lay person who ministers in a new language area.

People who have oral history traditions memorize quickly without written aids, so if the seekers are illiterate they can still learn vast portions of the Scriptures in their language. One problem, though, which the Christian worker consistently encounters is the problem of people understanding the Scriptures in thier heart language. Leaders must be aware that memorization is possible without comprehension.

Translating pertinent verses or portions into several languages may be necessary to meet the needs of a mixed group. The use of a trade language is only acceptable if the people use the trade language in their homes for "living." All translations used in the work must be cross-examined by more than one person to make certain that the meanings are clear. Even small linguistic errors can result in miscomprehension and spiritual disaster. Scriptures which are memorized with understanding can feed the soul and produce much fruit.

3. Use lay witnesses for cross-fertilization with testimonies. People using this ministry in adjacent churches will benefit greatly by sharing experiences of victory over sorcery. The beliefs in sorcery are quite uniform, but the experiences of persons involved in sorcery are always unique. The experiences of deliverance and faith are always encouraging to others who are struggling to gain the victory of faith over sorcery.

Witnessing should be a joyous by-product of victory through faith in Jesus Christ and a heart filled with the Holy Spirit, and it is expected that the most effective witnessing will be done among families, clans, and friends. Those who know the converts best will listen with interest to their strange tale of freedom from sorcery. While such sharing is expected to be spontaneous, each person who makes a decision for Christ must be encouraged to witness effectively. This witnessing can take place in a formal way in a church service, or it may be done spontaneously on the street, or even planned carefully for a one-on-one confrontation. Witnessing can both encourage maturing Christians as well as create interest among the unchurched people. If the person who makes the witness is genuine, then his testimony will be effective in any group of people because the Holy Spirit will bless it.

4. Expect power encounters and ocular demonstrations involving new converts. Any time a person moves toward God and is genuinely converted, the old forms of Satan's power will bring oppostion from the start. Sooner or later there will need to be some encounter between the power of God and the power of Satan. This may occur in a ceremonial burning of fetishes and "medicines," or it may develop from a planned breaking of some rule which relates to sorcery. This is not something which is to be conjured up. It needs to flow naturally from the experience of a full heart as guided by the Holy Spirit.

When a decision is made by a Christian to contest the evil powers, then as many persons as possible should observe it. The entire event should be based on the testimony of a delivered one, so that even those who observe from a distance will be able to understand that God's power, acting through the Holy Spirit, is greater than Satan's. A public crisis of this sort, which can be observed by other people, will help to encourage both the observers and the participant, because it confirms that the person who was involved in sorcery has been changed by faith in Jesus Christ.

These valuable, courageous acts have sometimes been disregarded as fanatical, or acted out without the benefit of enough viewers. Both of these errors need to be avoided. We recall one incident of a Congo missionary who went up a forbidden mountain of the spirits at Sambisamb, and note that the same act by a victorious Congolese Christian, with more observers, would have done much more for the kingdom of God.

5. Pay special attention to unusually receptive groups. In general, one finds that when people are moved to new surroundings, they become more receptive to new ideas. The old fetishes, sorcery fears, and idols are, at least in part, left behind. They are suddenly vulnerable to new ideas in an unusual way. To illustrate, a youth moving to a big center for secondary school may find that enough of his old ties have been cut so as to free him from the old patterns that dominated his thinking and believing. Also, patients in the hospitals are suddenly out of the usual routines of life and thus they often become more open to the gospel in a new way. However, extreme fears concerning sorcery often accompany illness and snake bites. Such fears may or may not make patients more open to the gospel. Refugees and job seekers are more open to ministry, too.

Thus, in each community there will be groups where sowing the seed of God's Word is easier than in others. These groups may or may not show up in the survey questionnaires used in preparation, because they often appear suddenly in a community and then return to their villages after receiving help.

In any of these groups, the leaders are important. Chiefs or spokespersons for any group of people will have special influence on others if they can be reached. If they can be approached and won first, it may prevent an attitude that the gospel is for "lesser" people.

6. Present scientific evidence to discount sorcery. Evidence that is contrary to the claims of sorcery is useful for two reasons. In the first place, timely explanations and scientific proofs will cause doubts among those who are trapped by sorcery. This is not the same as delivering them from sorcery, but it can be a tool used to explain the world which God has created. In this way deception loses some of its grip and a door may be opened to present the

Scriptures.

A second use of scientific evidence is to encourage believers so they can understand their world better. For example, a victorious Christian medical doctor can explain causes of diseases and the results of medicines. Once sorcery-bound people have taken a step in faith and found release by grace, they are no longer compelled to find the hidden sorcery cause for the explainable events. They are then free to understand the facts when they are presented in comprehensible terms. Secular knowledge alone cannot free people from sorcery, but when it is used in connection with the power of the Holy Spirit, it can be of great assistance in pushing sorcery further from the believer.

This tool may be very effective with youths who are eager to learn and want to understand. We previously quoted Mbuya's statement that modern youths wanted to learn both secular knowledge and sorcery at the same time. This situation presents a challenge to Christians to show the incompatability of the two positions. Only the Holy Spirit can reveal this truth; therefore, a faithful presentation of the Scriptures must accompany any attempt to reach such youths.

17

CULTURAL FOLLOW-UPS WITH CHRISTIAN SUBSTITUTES

As the community of victorious Christians grows in numbers, there will be opportunity for Christians to adjust to their own culture. These adjustments will enable Christians to be an integral part of the culture without being victims of the sorcery influences. Likewise, Christians can influence cultural changes that will bring blessings to the entire community. Such changes should be carefully considered and prayerfully developed so that no helpful part of the culture is lost.

Those who have genuine conversion experiences will leave the evil practices behind and then be free spiritually to construct some substitutes for their former sinful practices. These should include the following:

1. Substitute the Scriptures for divination. Divination is the practice of magic to discover something hidden or secret or in the future. The Christian has no use for magic in any form, but each one does need the guidance of God for his life. Practical Bible studies for believers can include guides to verses that help in times of sorrow, times of need, times of fear, and times of joy. The list can continue, but the point is, that where divination met a need in the person's life before conversion, now scriptural references can be substituted in place of divination to meet those same needs. However, be aware of a tendency to use the Bible as a magic charm for protection and to allay fears. This is a common syncretistic trap.

2. Develop memorial services to replace ancestor worship or contact with the deceased. As people turn from sorcery to Jesus as their Saviour, the Holy Spirit is their power. In this new faith, they will discover that the old fears and idolatry related to the ancestors must be set aside or their faith will be destroyed. However, it is extremely difficult to cast aside all their ties to the deceased. Therefore, with careful Scriptural guidance, there can be a time of remembering and of sharing with their family the memories of past experiences with deceased relatives.

This should not be left to the devices of each individual, however, because of the danger of syncretism. It must rather be a prayerfully developed substitute that will have special meaning to the converted and thus fill the vacancy left by ancestor worship. Part of this should be a service in the church where mutual encouragement is nurtured. Another part should be in the home and include the extended family. If that causes problems, it should include only the members of the family who are open to the Christian faith. Such services may also be a strong witness among the non-Christians.

This memorial service may include prayers of thanksgiving for those who were once with the family, as well as looking at pictures, if they are available, to refresh memories, and a time of sharing the meaning of this event with the children and youths of the family. There must be no prayers to the deceased or attempts to contact them. An offering might be given to the work of the Lord in memory of the deceased. Careful guidance is needed to distinguish each act from its sorcery-influenced counterpart; however, this must be carefully worked out in advance, because a quick and shallow treatment of this substitute may return sorcery to its former place in the believer's life.

3. Replace protective fetishes and "medicines" with the dedication of homes and family. Fetishes are used to manipulate spiritual power for protection or for special help. This protection and special help are provided by the abiding Christ and the indwelling Holy Spirit for the believer. The Psalmist looked to God for protection and help. Jesus prayed for God's will to be done, but he sought the help of God the Father to do it. Christians have every scriptural right to call upon God in the name of Jesus Christ to protect their home and their family within God's perfect will. At the

same time they need to realize that physical protection is secondary to spiritual protection from the "wiles of the devil." The power of the Holy Spirit which is available for those who believe is grossly neglected, and sorcery has reclaimed many because of overwhelming fear and a feeling of helplessness. Fetishes provided an object of trust, but the Holy Spirit whom Jesus sends is to be that object of trust for a Christian. Dedicating homes, young children, older children going away to school, and any who have a special responsibility makes a transition to greater trust and assurance in Christ than they had previously in any fetish. Where this is not a practice of the Church, it should be instigated as part of a comprehensive plan to give wholeness to the experience of finding Christ.

4. Instigate thanksgiving rituals at harvest time and at the first rain. Public rituals involving praise and thanksgiving for what God has provided in his creation should be substituted for any fertility rituals or any ritual aimed at controlling nature. Sorcery has often been closely related to nature, so these Christian rituals can help people to relate their extreme efforts for survival to God's blessings in nature. Where fertility rituals were performed out of fear and obligation, now thanksgiving rituals can be an expression of gratitude and joy.

Praising the Lord has always resulted in blessings; hence the animistic people must not miss this opportunity. Therefore, two things must be kept in mind. First, the Scriptures instruct us: "Speak to one another with psalms, hymns and spiritual songs. Sing and make music in your heart to the Lord...." This is a simple matter of overflowing during good times. There is, however, another part of the instruction given which says: "...always giving thanks to God the father for everything, in the name of our Lord Jesus Christ."[1] The "always" includes crop failures, storms, and disasters, along with the blessed events of life, and this must be carefully taught to the Christians. Would-be Christians feel lost in difficult times, so they revert immediately to magic and sorcery. There must be much teaching about continuous thanksgiving in preparation for a victorious Christian life.

The second thing to keep in mind is that the Christians should pray, making their requests known to God. This includes requests for good crops and rain, but it can also mean praying for different kinds of crops so they can feed their children better.

On one Congo mission station local non-Christians said that expensive well drilling for water failed because the spirits in the hills were displeased. The Christians joined in prayer, requesting the much needed water, and the next day the drillers found abundant water at a more shallow level than expected.

Also, in another area, a victorious former prostitute had the best garden in a huge village. She often told fellow gardeners: "You must become a Christian to have a good garden!" The Lord had given her new ideas, new goals, and a new heart to till her garden. God is certainly interested in the lives and the families of his children, so they should openly commune with him. The Christian faith is so much more practical than most dare to believe!

5. Introduce (or re-introduce) Christian marriage to replace live-ins and polygamy. In many animistic cultures there are very few Christian marriages, so sorcery has a great opportunities through temporary "marriage" agreements and childlessness. The victorious Christian who emerges from sorcery bondage must be aided to see that the plan of God includes families and marriage.

Once more, the Scriptures must be our guide. They speak clearly and precisely concerning marriage and morals. What is lacking in specific statements forbidding polygamy is amply made up for with disastrous illustrations of polygamy, inferences to immorality, and specific moral demands. Certainly the underlying intent revealed in the Scriptures is monogamy. These are not to be passed over lightly, but taught with understanding.

No new Christian can survive sorcery without a clear conviction of the soundness of Christian marriage as outlined in the Bible. Some victorious Christians who understand the Scriptures have been observed to accept monogamy spontaneously and joyfully!

Childlessness is a horror and disaster for many animists; it is considered the direct result of sorcery. All barrenness is considered to be caused by sorcery, and attempts to overcome childlessness usually involve sorcery. For Christians, children are considered blessings, but there is no stigma attached to childlessness. Therefore, if childless couples desire children, let them seek help through proper medical channels and through prayer. If there still are no children, then the couple should seek the lesson God has for them in this situation, as well as their place in the body of

Christ. Mutual encouragement could be of great help if there is more than one couple who faces this problem. One childless Christian couple in Congo opened their home to receive several children who were orphaned by the death of a close relative.

A prayer group with a focus on selfless service to help needy children could be a beginning. This could help establish the couple's faith in the power of the Holy Spirit to replace the necessity of bearing children.

6. Form small prayer cells that will replace the gossip circles which flourish among the people groups. Every temptation and every problem faced by a new Christian will be aggravated by gossip. Visits with relatives, inactivity during the tropical storms, the long walks to the gardens—all of these and many more present opportunities for gossip. The most useful tool against this is prayer. Each convert should not only be involved in a church, but also be in a smaller, more personal prayer group. There personal needs, as well as the problems of the community, can be shared and lifted to God in prayer.

For example, most villages of Southern Congo have a small, round, grass roof supported by several poles which resembles a one room hut with no walls. Its size varies from space for six people to twelve people or more. Men sit under these roofs for the shade, protected from the hot sun, or on a rainy day they will huddle forward to warm themselves around glowing coals. This structure provides a place to discuss the hunts, the women, the crops, or any other topic. In contrast, Christians usually go into a closed room to pray. It is possible that the grass-roofed meeting place would provide adequate privacy, reduce suspicions of non-Christians, and free the Christians to share in prayer on a deeper level.

7. Develop local Christian music to replace the anti-Christian dancing music. As new Christians turn to the Church, the music which they find there is too often foreign to them. A translated hymn can grow into a blessing, but it may not be a natural expression from the heart. Some of the tribes have different octaves than others and different tastes in music. Therefore, as God gives talent, local Christians should be encouraged to develop sacred music from the heart. A saved heart needs to sing, and a life delivered from sorcery needs to praise. These experiences expressed in the local rhythm and beat could be extremely powerful weapons

against sorcery. We recall that the Wesleys very successfully used music from the bars with new Christian words!

To summarize these points—there is need for cultural follow-up so Christians can experience a whole life in Christ. The late Donald McGavran, a noted authority on church growth, wrote:

> The Holy Spirit and the Bible are living powerful forces. I suggest that the older churches may well allow some beginning adjustments which seem wrong to them, as long as the Bible is accepted as the sole authority in life and worship.[2]

Certainly no one is converted into instant perfection, for the Scriptures teach us that we all need to grow into maturity (see Eph. 4). While acknowledging these truths, we must never lose sight of the goal of perfection, of holiness before the Lord.

---

[1] Eph. 5:19-20.

[2] Donald McGavran, *The Clash Between Christianity and Cultures* (Washington, D.C.: Canon Press, 1974), p. 28.

18

CONCLUSIONS
AND CAUTIONS

Most of the above material has been directed to those who need Jesus Christ as Saviour and Deliverer, but a word needs to be said concerning those who carry out this ministry to the sorcery-bound people.

Support Ministry Needed

Once the pattern of ministry is established, spontaneous sharing and praying should be encouraged. It is most important that those who are working and witnessing against sorcery must have spiritual support to continue. Satan will not leave them alone for long as he sees his territory threatened and conquered by effective ministry. Joyful sharing and meaningful fellowship will do much to keep them victorious.

Since there is great danger in over-organization, it is doubtful that a "program" as such would be helpful. However, when there is more than one person working in such ministry there should be a coordinator who can encourage them to have regular times of prayer and fellowship together. Facing the problems alone can be very difficult and eventually cause them to lose interest or motivation. Therefore, if possible, two or more need to work together, following carefully the local codes of behaviour, i.e. men with men, women with women, teachers with teachers, etc.

If a Christian worker is alone, his failure to win a seeker after much effort and prayer can lead to discouragement or despondency. Sharing such problems not only lifts the burden off a weary brother, it also brings new insights and ideas to enhance the work of fellow ministers (laity or clergy).

This ministry has nothing to do with monetary support. This work will need to flow from a full, blessed heart and not from any aspirations of gain. Thus, it is expected that each minister continue his regular duties or job and reach out voluntarily to the receptive ones in his circle of family and friends. Salary or benefits can negatively motivate a person by a desire for gain.

Some Cautions to be Observed

There are four cautions to be expressed in relation to this ministry to those bound by sorcery. They all stem from the extreme seriousness of the problem which faces these people. Because sorcery has ruled supreme in many areas for centuries, it will not be surrendered easily. It is well established and has been highly refined as a tool of Satan. Therefore, one must tread carefully with these cautions in mind:

1. Plan to complete the ministry once it is begun. Too many "projects" of evangelism have been started and not completed. This not only leaves the seekers without spiritual victory, but worse than that, it often leaves them with a confused heart and closed mind to further efforts to win them to Jesus Christ. Many have been innoculated against genuine Christian faith because of half-hearted efforts to win them. This ministry should begin with the full understanding that it will be continued over a length of time. The actual schedule is not important, but steady progress should be envisioned toward the goal of a whole Christian person filled with the Holy Spirit.

2. Pay close attention to timing. When people are open and receptive to this ministry the time is right to begin. Conversely, when there is little interest or concern about freedom from sorcery, the timing is wrong. Work in such instances may be limited to pre-ministry approaches that will open the way to effective contact in the future.

The amount of time spent on the different steps or procedures is not important (the order is important). For some it may take more time to work through the Biblical treatment of sorcery, while for others more time may be needed to develop a readiness for the step of faith. That is no problem; therefore, the amount of time should be adjusted to the person or persons being ministered to.

As long as there is steady progress there is no incorrect timing.

3. Be aware of dissonance and plan to minister to it. Hesselgrave defines dissonance for us:

> Applied to the conversion process, dissonance refers to that period during which the new convert encounters the various difficulties that accrue to following Christ in the cultural contexts of non-Christian traditions.[1]

This problem is extremely severe when a new Christian suddenly finds pressures from family members, from the sorcerers, and from old fears or fetishes which are constantly close at hand. Doubts will suddenly come concerning his conversion and there will be strong temptations to return to sorcery. According to Hesselgrave this is most likely to happen during the first forty-eight hours following the decision to follow Christ. If the converts are left to their own devices they may fall, but if they are supported by fellow Christians there is no reason for failure.

This support must include prayer, Scripture reading, especially sharing the passages on assurance, and a reasonable perspective of the past and the future. Such a perspective will help the newly-won people to understand what they have been saved from and what lies before them in the faith. An all night praise and prayer meeting will give strength to the beginner and would fit many animistic cultural patterns for dealing with serious problems.

Any combination of helps can be used if the distinct goal is a continuous growth toward maturity in Jesus Christ.

4. Avoid shortcuts. This was mentioned earlier, but it must be considered in light of the entire ministry as proposed. Animistic people are not time-oriented, but event-oriented. In ministry, this means that regardless of the time involved, any event in progress should be completed. There is a logical and reasonable progression through the chapters in Part II, and as the Scriptures are used in this way they build on each other.

The danger of shortcuts comes mostly from missionaries who are only oriented to the western world view, and others who have been educated into a world view which differs from that of the local people. Impatience in any who attempt this ministry will be disastrous to the seekers.

To conclude, let us listen to Mbiti. In an article on African concepts of Christology he writes:

> The greatest need among African peoples, is to see, to know, and experience Jesus Christ as the victor over the powers and forces from which Africa knows no means of deliverance. It is for this reason that they show special interest in the Temptation of Jesus and his victory over the devil through the power of the Holy Spirit. They know that the devil is not just an academic problem but a reality, manifesting his power through ways such as unwanted spirit possessions, sickness, madness, discord, fights, murderers, and so on.[2]

This ministry is prayerfully prepared for meeting this need as stated by Mbiti. There is no other possibility for deliverance, but with God's perfect plan there is no need for another.

---

1 Hesselgrave, *Communicating Christ*, p. 450.

2 Mbiti, "Some African Concepts of Christology," in *Christ and the Younger Churches*, ed. Georg F. Vicedom (London: S.P.C.K., 1972), p. 55.

APPENDIX I

Questionnaire 1
Questionnaire for Pastors to Study Traditional Religion

God

1. What is the traditional name for God among your people?

   _____

2. Who prays to that God? _____

3. What do they pray for? _____

4. Does God answer these traditional prayers? _____

5. Are there any intermediaries between God and man? ____

Ancestors

1. Where are the deceased after they die? _____

2. What influence do they have? _____

3. Which ancestor is most important? _____

4. Are ancestors used by sorcerers for evil acts against other people? _____

5. Are ancestors reincarnated? _____

Rituals

1. What rituals are observed? _____

2. Which rituals are centered in life? _____

   Which in death? _____

3. What sacrifices are offered? _____

4. Who officiates or leads the rituals? _____

5. Are sorcery and rituals related? _____

Sacrifices

1. Why are sacrifices made?_____

2. Is sorcery a part of all sacrifices? _____

3. What powers are involved in sacrifice? _____

4. Name the sacrifices you know about? _____

5. Who participates in any particular sacrifice?_____

Sorcery

1. Who died this month (or year) from sorcery? _____

2. In your village how many have sorcery power?
(no names)_____

3. What stops the power of sorcery? _____

4. Could your village live without sorcery? _____

5. Would you pay to get rid of all sorcery? _____

Illness

1. Where does illness come from? _____

2. Who in this village can cure illness? _____

3. Does hospital medicine have power?_____

4. What diseases are incurable by hospital medicine? _____

5. Is sorcery illness and physical illness different?_____

Fetishes

1. Name the fetishes in your village. _____

2. Are fetishes connected with sorcery? _____

3. How are fetishes obtained? _____

4. Can fetishes be discarded after purchase? _____

5. Do some villagers live without any fetishes? _____

Personal Information:

Married? ❑ Christian wedding ❑ Village wedding ❑

I have had: one wife ❑ two wives ❑ more ❑

My age: ❑ youth ❑ middle age ❑ older ❑

I attended school _____years.

Bibles: are available ❑ are not available ❑

I live in: city ❑ small village ❑ large village ❑

Questionnaire 2

1. I believe in a Supreme God. Yes ❑ No ❑ Not sure ❑

2. There are many invisible powers around me.
   Yes ❑ No ❑ Not sure ❑

3. Everything I can see has a spirit. Yes ❑ No ❑ Not sure ❑

4. I trust fetishes to help me. Yes ❑ No ❑ Sometimes ❑

5. Everyone believes in sorcery. Yes ❑ No ❑ Not sure ❑

6. I am afraid at night. Yes ❑ No ❑ Sometimes ❑

7. Other people can kill me with sorcery.
   Yes ❑ No ❑ Not sure ❑

8. I have enemies who do not like me.
   Yes ❑ No ❑ Not sure ❑

9. My ancestors cause me to fear. Yes ❑ No ❑ Not sure ❑

10. I would like help to be free of fear.
    Yes ❑ No ❑ Not sure ❑

11. Sorcery is my big problem. Yes ❑ No ❑ Not sure ❑

12. The Holy Spirit gives power to help Christians.
    Yes ❑ No ❑ Not sure ❑

13. God can help people. Yes ❑ No ❑ Not sure ❑

14. Evil spirits prevent God's work. Yes ❑ No ❑ Not sure ❑

15. Satan is head of the evil spirits. Yes ❑ No ❑ Not sure ❑

16. I am now a Christian. Yes ❑ No ❑ Not sure ❑

17. Sin is my problem. Yes ❑ No ❑ Not sure ❑

18. I know people who want to become Christians.
Yes ❑ No ❑

19. Sorcerers help people with sorcery.
Yes ❑ No ❑ Sometimes ❑

20. Fetishes are helpful to Christians.
Yes ❑ No ❑ Sometimes ❑

21. I can read the Bible. Yes ❑ No ❑

22. Pastors are helpful leaders. Yes ❑ No ❑ Some ❑

23. I want to become a Christian. Yes ❑ No ❑

24. I am afraid to become a Christian. Yes ❑ No ❑

25. Sorcery opposes Christianity. Yes ❑ No ❑

26. Jesus Christ died to forgive everyone's sin. Yes ❑ No ❑

27. Christians can sin and still be saved. Yes ❑ No ❑

28. Jesus Christ delivered me from fear of sorcery. Yes ❑ No ❑

29. The thing which causes me the most fear is _____

30. I suggest for ministering to the sorcery-bound people____

I am:
❑ Man   ❑ Youth   ❑ Older
❑ Woman   ❑ Middle aged

I have:
❑ Joined a church ❑ Refused any church
❑ Visited church

My education:
- ❑ Primary school
- ❑ University
- ❑ Jr. High
- ❑ High School
- ❑ Seminary

I live:
- ❑ In a city
- ❑ In a village

Questionnaire 3

For Use by Interviewers

1. Sorcery is a serious problem.
   - A. For me ☐
   - B. For some ☐
   - C. Only in the past ☐
   - D. Not really ☐

2. Who was Jesus Christ?
   - A. Prophet ☐
   - B. Saviour ☐
   - C. Good man ☐
   - D. Other_____

3. What do you think of the Bible?
   - A. Good Book ☐
   - B. God's Word ☐
   - C. History
   - D. Other_____

4. Sorcery powers can be overcome by
   - A. Medicine ☐
   - B. Magic only ☐
   - C. Faith in Jesus Christ
   - D. Other_____

5. My opinion of Christianity
   - A. OK for others ☐
   - B. Best for me ☐
   - C. A fake belief ☐
   - D. Other_____

6. Christians can use sorcery.
   - A. Never ☐
   - B. Any time ☐
   - C. In special need ☐
   - D. Other_____

Male_____ Female_____

Rural_____ Urban_____

Youth_____ Adult_____

Questionnaire 4

Bible Knowledge Related to Sorcery

1. The Bible is available in any language.
   Yes ❑ No ❑ Don't know ❑

2. I have a Bible, or a portion of the Bible.
   Yes ❑ No ❑ Language _____

3. The Bible is good for all people.
   Yes ❑ No ❑ Maybe ❑

4. Sorcery is mentioned in the Bible.
   Yes ❑ No ❑ Don't know ❑

5. God hates sorcery.
   Yes ❑ No ❑ Don't know ❑

6. Samuel went to a sorcerer.
   True ❑ False ❑ Don't know ❑

7. God's power is greater than any sorcerer.
   True ❑ False ❑ Don't know ❑

8. The New Testament says Satan causes sorcery.
   True ❑ False ❑ Don't know ❑

9. The Bible tells that all sorcery will be destroyed by God.
   True ❑ False ❑ Don't know ❑

10. Christians are permitted to use sorcery.
    True ❑ False ❑ Don't know ❑

11. The Bible was written by:
    Many authors ❑   God himself ❑
    One author ❑   Don't know ❑

12. Jesus Christ was:

    A prophet ❑   Only a man ❑

    Saviour ❑   Don't know ❑

13. Sin causes: Death ❑ Life ❑ Don't know ❑

14. Sorcery is:

    Necessary ❑   Useful ❑

    Harmful ❑   Undecided ❑

15. The power of the Holy Spirit is:

    More than sorcery power   ❑

    Less than sorcery power   ❑

    Don't know   ❑

16. I would like God to help me in this way:_____

_____

17. I would like to learn more about: _____

18. I am afraid of:

    Darkness ❑   Sorcery ❑

    Spirits ❑   Parents ❑

    Ancestors ❑   Animals ❑

19. I have seen:

    Sorcerers ❑   Visions ❑

    Spirits ❑   Dreams ❑

20. Faith in Jesus Christ brings:

    Forgiveness of sin ❑   Good luck ❑

    More money ❑   Nothing special ❑

21. Our evil comes from:

    Adam and Eve ❑   Each person ❑

    God ❑   Evil spirits ❑

I am: Male ❑   Female ❑

I finished: Primary school_____

I am in primary school_____

I am in secondary school_____

I quit school at _____grade.

I live in: A city_____ A village_____

I have: Less than 15 years_____

      Between 15 and 20 years_____

      Over 20 years_____

I am: Married_____ Single_____ Divorced_____

APPENDIX II
SORCERY FOR KILLING

Message by Mukalay wa Ngoi
Born in Ankoro, Nord Shaba, Zaire(now Republic of Congo)
Taped at Mulungwishi Seminary
by Elwood Bartlett
Edited by Marvin S. Wolford

When you give birth to a child, it is impossible to know what he will do in the future. Thus when I was a child I did not know that I would acquire "medicine". This "medicine" was my father's. When I was grown, my father died while I was in school. I did not know what had killed my father. At the time of my father's death, I was not able to eat any cooked food, nor any food roasted in the fire. If I tried to eat, I always vomited every time. I was only able to drink water.

Then my brothers and sisters (extended family) said, "Perhaps this child Mukalay is the one who killed his father. Why would this child Mukalay begin to waste away this way?" So the elders took their money and we went to a diviner, one who could know the hidden secrets. That diviner told them that this child Mukalay was not the one who killed his father. He added that it was the "medicine" left by his father that was following Mukalay. The elders did not want to tell me everything openly. However, our whole family just knew that Mukalay was the child that would be receiving all the "medicine" of sorcery left by my father.

Then one day I saw a group of people called *bulumbu* (Luba) or *chiyembok* (Uruund). They totaled eight people altogether, and they had all their things used for sorcery and their drums too. They were all very old. In the morning, they called me to come, and sat me in the midst of them. They began to beat their drums and sing. While they sang they closed my eyes and all my thoughts were lost, and I didn't know anything at all. I felt like a person who has drunk too much alcoholic beverage. That is the way the power of Satan appeared to me. The power of Satan is like that, it can take a person, turn him around and make him as if he were drunk from drinking too much.

When they had finished doing everything, they said to me, "Truly it is the *bulumbu* of your father that is following you." (In the sense that he was now a *bulumbu* like his father.)

I kept the "medicine" for eighteen years. In the year 1973 I went to Kamina (city) and the people came to me and said, "Let's go to Kamponda, because you, Mukalay, are a young man who knows how to divine very well. Come, because you, Mukalay, you tell us everything openly, and warn us not to make ourselves guilty by thinking wrongly about others. There is a man named Kamponda, and he called a killer in, instructed him to kill a certain man. That is how Kamponda has killed one of our relatives."

They then added, "Mukalay, now if you really do have true 'medicine' for sorcery, go and kill that man." I was very surprised when I realized what they were asking of me. Then the chief of the village of Nkinda told me, "Mukalay, you are just a young child. Don't agree to this thing, for you will only get killed. This man Kamponda has killed many people."

Then I answered Chief Nkinda, "My eyes have seen the very big ocean, I cannot be surprised at the width of the Lualaba river." I told him that I was going to see Kamponda, to see if he really did have more sorcery power than I had. But in my heart I thought I had a very great power of sorcery, and decided that if Kamponda did indeed have more power and could actually kill me, fine, then let it happen. I did not want to hear about others who had more sorcery power than I; I had to try the power to test it. Thus Chief Nkinda said to go ahead.

All the time that I was planning to do all these things, God was arranging a time when I would be saved and delivered from evil. When I got to Luena, I slept in a house there, and made ready all the "medicine" for this man, Kamponda. I killed Kamponda. That is the reason I came to Luena.

As I sat and pondered all this, I decided I would go to the church. I carried all my sorcery "medicines" and brought them to the church in Mpande, Zaire (now Congo). Before this I had watched some of the believing Christians, and then had asked them if they would agree for me to join the church with my tobacco, and my liquor, and my sorcery. If they would agree to that, then I would become a believer.

That night I went in the house to sleep. I saw four people that are called angels, in Kiluba we say *ba-Mutole*. These four stood beside me, two on each side with me in the middle. These four said to me, "Mukalay, take off your black cloak, and take this white cloak from us and put it on now." Then they grabbed hold of me on each side and they clothed me with the white cloak. Then they said, "Today, go to the church, believe, and follow me. But never again do any of your sorcery, for if you do, you will die." This terrified me, because they said that I would die if ever again I did any sorcery.

When I got up in the morning, I went to the church. There some of the people knew me from my visit the day before. Some of the others said, "Definitely not!" They all began to sing, but not me. I just sat and looked around. What I wanted was for the church to agree for me to drink my liquor. When they finished singing I stood in the midst of them and said, "Today I have come to believe, and to follow God."

When the people heard this they were very happy. They did not know that I had evil sorcery "medicine" for killing people, because few of the people knew me. So I told them myself that I was a murdering sorcerer. Some teachers of the CEM from Mbandaka were elated, and began to pray for me. Then they took me to Pastor Lubinga, who received me with prayer and thanksgiving. Then they said, "Why has God brought us a man like this one?"

They asked me my name, and when they heard it they said, "Now you must stay here, because we are afraid that if you return to your home you will return to your sorcery." I stayed with them, and they had the task of teaching me the Word of God right from the time I believed. That is how God took me out of evil, and now I know I belong to God.

Truly, you must genuinely follow God, for He certainly exists. I, Mukalay, was a devil. From the time my mother bore me, I did nothing else. My work was to eat up (to waste) the money of other people with false "medicine". Any diviner or any other person who makes other sorcery "medicine" are deceivers with many lies. They do it to get the money from others for nothing—do not follow them, for they are liars!…I, Mukalay, wasted the lives of many people by killing them, and never did these eyes of mine shed tears.

Q: You said that the carved buffalo was the diviner? The thing I want to know is this: the elders gave you this "medicine". They said you would inherit the sorcery power of your father who died, then they gave you this carved buffalo with the whitewash and the chicken head inside. Did these things give you the power of sorcery?

A: When they gave me that thing, they also gave me things to drink made from trees they had cooked up and sap from other trees. But I cannot explain the things they did to me.

Q: When they called you to divine or to make "medicine", if the village was some distance from you and you didn't know the people there, how did you know who the person was who was causing the illness or trying to kill a person? Don't answer as a believer in Christ, but answer as you were in the beginning.

A: Many people have perished in the path of sorcery and divination. Many people want to get other people's money for nothing. You must realize that an anti-sorcery person, or a healer is actually a judge for the people. When one of them asks you the first question then he listens carefully to find a good way to answer you. You yourself give him a way to get your money for nothing. I would listen very carefully to your answers to my questions and find a way to follow your answers right up to the last. Then you would think I had really told you something valuable.

Q: If a sorcerer wants to kill someone, is there a way that the victim can pay the sorcerer or give him something else so he can live?

A: Yes, if the victim has something to give the sorcerer, he can save himself. He can also give a person from his family and thus save himself.... Some of the people will agree that a person has sorcery power because of their fear, and they become horrified, but truly it isn't his at all. They don't know anything at all, but because of the fear of the people the exorcist can hide his "medicine" in a bottle, or a horn, or whatever in some place. Then he will say "go over to that particular place, there is a certain thing there." When the people go and find the stuff there, then they agree that all the sorcery and anti-sorcery is true because they didn't know when I put it there. This is why I have to have other living people help me do this sort of thing. The main thing, it is all for money.

Believers, don't be amazed at these things. Don't pay them any heed or repeat them, for some who have not seen the process of exorcising sorcery, when they see these deceitful things, may quickly believe them and give them credence. Let the others with true faith stand firm in their faith in God, and not look upon the lies of Satan. I, Mukalay, have spent 18 years in these things. But now I know that truly God exists, and that He has the greatest power.

Q: If you get dirt from my footprint and a piece of cloth from my clothes, then in a short time I move and go a long distance away, how can your "medicine" follow me?

A: I already have things that belong to your body, then the things that I make to kill you are really yours. They tell that a dead person is a spirit, like the mind, and it is certainly true. The power comes from that spirit of the deceased. The spirit I have works for me. I will give to the spirit all the things that belong to you. Even if you go far away the spirit will go and find you in five days. So then, anywhere you go, to a bar, or on a trip, you will definitely meet with him, and he will most certainly kill you.

If after five days he hasn't found you, that spirit will return and say, "I didn't find him." So I will then go find another spirit to go find you. I take him to the place where you used to be. At that time you would die just like a chicken.

Q: You, Mukalay, said that everything is deception, so is the story you just told us deceit also?

A: I answer many things and lies and deceit are in the answers. It is a way of telling it just as if I really did want to remove the sorcery power from another person. Many of those things are lies and deceit just because of making money.

It was deceit when I told about the sorcery power I took away from a person. The person who did the hiding of things or dropped things in the hole where I told them to dig is a man who lives with me. I sent him by another name to deceive just like I told you. If I deceive you here now, it is just to get your money.

Q: Then was the explanation of killing a person also deceit?

A: No, the things about killing people are all true—that is what I was doing. I cannot send a spirit off (to work for me) for nothing, I must pay him something. These things I did as well as taking the sorcery of another person.

As concerns the sorcery for killing. If God hadn't removed me from sorcery, and if I hadn't taken all my things to the elders of the church, I could do all the things one by one for you to see. Perhaps you would even be frightened to see it and be very amazed. The sorcery for killing is certainly a reality. I have killed many people. Many were destroyed by death.

Q: You said that if a person dies with genuine faith, you sorcerers could not call him back with sorcery, or even know the place where he had gone, or even see him. Now what if a person was prayed for as we have heard about just now, what will happen to him?

A: I said that one who truly believes with genuine faith in God,

226

when he dies, if we call his spirit, we cannot find it or know the place where his spirit is. However, a false believer, or if they pray for him and sing for him after he is dead, then we sorcerers can call him, and he will gladly agree because he has no place to go. His spirit just stays on earth, so when we call he answers willingly.

Q: In our village they tell us that some who have died return to the village. Do you know about this, and have you ever tried to catch a spirit in a village?

A: I will tell you that there is not a single village without a spirit staying there. In all villages, spirits are there. The spirits come more often to the village in the rainy times.

APPENDIX III
Interview with Bishop Ngoi Wakadilo
Scarritt College, Nashville, Tenn.
May 29, 1979
Edited by Marvin S. Wolford

Basic information: The late Bishop Ngoi Wakadilo was the leader of the United Methodist Church in North Shaba, Zaire (now Republic of Congo). He was formerly the bishop of the Southern Zaire Conference as well, his position at the time of this interview. He had been a pastor and District Superintendent as well as directing the Theological Seminary at Mulungwishi while teaching there. As an evangelical he was courageous in strengthening the spiritual and moral fiber of the Church. His strong personal faith and a genuine sense of humility gave him strength of leadership.

Q: Bishop, could you please express some of your insights on the problem of sorcery in the Southern Zaire area where you serve the Church?

A: The problem of sorcery is both complex and difficult. It is the old way of doing things. To begin with, we believed in a power that was evil, that is it could be used to cause harm to someone. This power was not in the same sense of making people ill or attacking them. This is power in the spiritual sense that is accomplished with spirits, and it is always intended to do harm to someone. For example, a sorcerer can kill someone because he doesn't like them. This can be done both to one present with the sorcerer, and to one who is absent.

Q: Is it necessary for the victim to be seen or touched? Also, is "medicine" used such as poisons, etc.?

A: That depends on the kind of action being considered. Yes. Sometimes poison is used. It just depends. I remember about one man in particular who was involved in the death of my father. I remember when that man repented, and confessed participating in that. He confessed because my father was already dead and we children had grown up by then. This man had been a sorcerer, but it was not he who wanted to kill my father. He was contacted by a member of the family, and I mention him because he used visible materials to kill him. He used a mixture made with many different things. He used poison and also a substance to cause irritation. With this he then made a powder. There are several possibilities for using this. One is to put it above the door, and when you arrive and just touch the door, the powder falls on you and provokes an irritation. When you scratch the skin, then the poison is absorbed. There is also a poison which can be put on a woman's bed. Then when she is in bed, the irritation can be scratched in the same way, and she will be poisoned. However, generally speaking, sorcery has to do with the spirits.

Now then, for we who are Christians, we know that people do firmly believe in these things. They believe that certain things exist, they believe that sorcery between people exists, they believe that sorcerers can kill people, and that poisons are used. We know this because of those people who have repented and confessed to these things.

What do we Christians say then? We say that such sorcery power may or may not exist, but whatever, God is more powerful than all of it! He paralyzed all the power of the magicians of Pharaoh, and we know of no limit to the power of God, to those who cry, who cry totally and sincerely to Him, and put all their confidence in Him. For Christians, there is no limit to the power of God and we are always victorious in every situation like that. What can the poison do, and what can the power do? God takes our part. If He intervenes, these things will not happen, but if He does not, we will just die, and one day all the accounts will be balanced.

To be victorious over these things, there is need for a greater power spiritually. The people believe these things, and to influence them at all they must come to believe that there is a more powerful force than the sorcery they trust. However, if you tell them that such things do not truly exist, and then one day they see that they do exist, then they are lost. Perhaps they will encounter someone who will say, "I killed a certain person." This happens from time to time in the Pentecostal Church. One person came to Manono where the church was almost empty. The people did not want to come to church because of a certain spiritualist who was in the church. He was a Christian, but he said, "We have more than you have spiritually." It turned out that he too repented, and confessed to killing different ones of the church. He told of changing the communion elements which the pastor provided for other things, and the people did not see it happen. After the service when people were leaving, he said they too needed to do the same thing. These things do disturb the Church.

We hold that Christ is the Head of the Church, and that no person is divine or has divine powers. There are no spirits with power greater than Jesus. . . none. If spirits enter the church and disturb the church, then we do not truly believe in Christ. If we stand firm in our faith, then no demonic power can enter to bother the church.

Q: Do you believe that most of the pastors in the church now have the Power of God in their hearts and lives to overcome sorcery beliefs and to be victorious?

A: Faith is the main thing. We have plenty of pastors who are able to give a theological message based on intelligence, but without faith. You know there is preaching with faith and without faith. There are not a few pastors who would believe in the power of sorcery.

Q: Would you please comment on the Holy Spirit in all of this? Perhaps the first part of this question is, what about a new Christian who knows little of the Bible and who has heard little preaching to help him, and he is afraid?

A: I must confess the weakness of our Church in that the pastors do not read the Bible. The Bible times were about like the period we are in now in Africa, a period of believing the forces of evil. It treats the demonic powers and the powers of magic. In that period they received a Victor who was Reality, who before God made Himself of no Reality, who was more powerful, like God. It is God who is Almighty, who is the "real Reality" if I may use that term. The Bible condemns all sorcery and such, and states that clearly in Revelation. The Bible gives us a Gospel (truly the Word) that is living and powerful. The Bible presents us with a Word who is always manifested with power. Jesus was before the demons, and not one withstood him, because He had a power. This Jesus departed with the promise to be with you wherever you are. There was no word of Jesus that was just verbal, for it always was with power and was living. The history of Paul bears this out as a reality, and we need to believe that.

If we do believe that with a sincere faith, then we can go forth with confidence that if anything happens to us, we are in the hand of God. Therefore, why should we be afraid? If the Holy Spirit is moved from first place, that is the worst thing. Jesus told the disciples that the spirit was willing but the flesh was weak. But for us it is sometimes reversed...the flesh is willing to serve God, or interested in it, but the Spirit is gone...that is a great danger for us. What are we to do? That is an impossibility. How can one minister to the people and encourage them to believe in the power of God, when he believes in the power of evil? If you believe in nothing, you believe in the power of evil!

APPENDIX IV
First interview with Rev. Nshid Sampas
January 27, 1979
Edited by Marvin S. Wolford

Basic information: Rev. Nshid Sampas is an ordained United Methodist minister, and a full member of the Southern Congo Annual Conference. He has successfully pastored several churches, including the largest church in the conference with 2,350 members. He has been trained in Urbanism in Cameroon, and has visited Ghana and Nigeria. Since 1972 he has been trained and engaged in assisting in the translation of the Bible into his Uruund language. His strong faith, proven by many hardships and near encounters with death, based in Bible knowledge, and his own family background of anti-sorcery within the tribal setting join to qualify him to speak on the subject at hand. He perceives the crisis facing the Church, and he perceives equally clearly the only hope—Jesus Christ working through the dynamic of the Holy Spirit.

Q: What really is sorcery to the Aruund people?

A: It is an invisible force which cannot be seen by the people, and usually does not involve "medicines" or poisons.

Q: Where does the power for sorcery come from?

A: The power begins with ancestors who had *ulaj*, or the power of sorcery.

Q: Who are the sorcerers?

A: Usually they are the elders, old men, women, or chiefs.

Third interview with Rev. Nshid Sampas
February 8, 1979
Edited by Marvin S. Wolford

Q: Can this spirit or power of sorcery be seen?

A: No, it is never visible.

Q: Is this power more effective close by, and does it decrease with longer distances?

A: Yes, the power is more dangerous close by, and to flee its effectiveness one would need to go some 150 miles or so to be safe. For example, a person afraid of sorcery power at Kapanga could be safe at Sandoa. (A distance of 150 miles.)

Q: Where does a sorcerer go after death?

A: All sorcerers must be burned. They are denied the respect of a burial, and this is the greatest disgrace for anyone. Then after they are burned, the spirit of the sorcerer is told to go away and never return. The intent is to send it to the *karung ka misiny* (the sea of the torturous grass) which is the Aruund concept of hell.

Q: Is there a name or a concept of Satan among the Aruund?

A: There is none. We do not have the idea of one single evil spirit being the source of all evil.

Q: Do mediums play any part in sorcery?

A: Mediums are not employed for the sake of talking with the deceased by sorcerers. One might use a medium to try to save himself by identifying another sorcerer through them, or sometimes the sorcerer might use a medium to work evil.

Q: Does the sorcerer use physical items to cause harm?

A: No, the power of sorcery is a spirit, and not physical.

Q: What relationship is seen between sorcery and illness?

A: All illness is considered to be caused by sorcery. Even if the disease is understood, still it is caused by sorcery. An epidemic that is wide-spread, or a famine is said to be caused by *Mwad a Neng*, and this is a special spirit that does this and is not really the work of sorcery as such.

Q: To repeat an earlier question, what is the base of sorcery, what makes it work?

A: The base is fear. No sorcery is effective without fear.

Fourth interview with Rev. Nshid Sampas (taped)
February 19, 1979
Edited by Marvin S. Wolford

Q: Has sorcery changed any in the years since independence?

A: I believe it is the same basically now as it was before independence (in 1960).

Q: Are their fears about the same as they were before?

A: Yes, I think so.

Q: Do you see any difference in "witchcraft" and in "sorcery?" To explain, I looked in the French dictionary and found "sorcery" listed as *sorcellerie*. Then they list under "witchcraft" the two terms, *sorcellerie* or *magie noire*.

A: *Magie noire* is our *ulaj*, or sorcery.

Q: In East Africa, I have read, there is a difference in sorcery and "good" magic. Do you also have that same sort of difference?

A: Yes, we have a difference. We have sorcery which is only *magie noire*, but we also have another. For example, if a person gets sick, they may go to a special person to get help.

Q: What is the name of that person, and do they use only "medicines" or do they use magic also?

A: That person is called *ngang*, and they use local African "medicines" as well as magic, or spirit power.

Q: You mentioned earlier that people are afraid of sorcery if they have offended someone or done something against them. Are they afraid then because of revenge?

A: They are afraid because another can do something bad to them. They are afraid for their own life.

Q: Does the sorcerer do something to them to make them ill or to actually kill them?

A: He will sometimes only make them ill with sorcery, and sometimes he will kill the victim.

Q: When a sorcerer makes someone ill, do they always intend for the victim to die?

A: No, not always. Sometimes they are not intended to die. For example, if the victim was only impolite, then they may just make him sick for that.

Q: Is there something else bad that a sorcerer will do to his victims other than make them ill?

A: Yes, perhaps the victim can't find a job. Or maybe he can't get married, or get along with other people.

Q: Are you saying, then, that virtually any kind of success can be prevented with sorcery?

A: Yes.

Q: Is death more often used than other kinds of evil treatment against the victim?

A: Yes, death is most often used.

Q: Are there certain people who cannot make accusations against another? That is to say, are certain relationships safe against sorcery use? For example, can a man and wife use sorcery against each other?

A: Not often in the case of man and wife, unless there is something very serious indeed, perhaps a death involved. As a rule they don't do it.

Q: What if the woman commits adultery?

A: Then in that case she may use sorcery against her husband.

Q: Why the wife, I thought it would be the husband who would use sorcery against her for her unfaithfulness?

A: Well, she might have her lover or another kill her husband in order to have freedom to do as she pleases. However, it might likewise be the husband who out of jealousy would use sorcery against his wife.

Q: What about chiefs, are they afraid of sorcery too?

A: Yes, definitely, because they are above other people (over other people). They have excessive fear of sorcery. I know of one chief (omitted) who walks with great fear. He looks constantly over his shoulders as he walks, he will refuse to drink water or to eat at another person's home. Fear especially comes to them because of others who could qualify for their chieftanship (children of chiefs), because these could get them killed in order to get the position of chief in their stead.

Q: Then is it true that anyone who is different in any way is fearful because of that "visibility?"

A: Yes, that is true, but there is a difference here. Those who are in a position of teaching are not so fearful of sorcery. Their fear comes from others who want to take their position away from them, not so much from sorcery. Those who fear sorcery most are those who are the ordinary people. If they are illiterate or if they are without much schooling or experience, then they are the ones who fear sorcery most. They fear it from others of their level, for they will feel jealousy or think evil if they are observing someone else raised up a bit or different.

Q: When there is trouble in the land, such as war time at independence, or the war times since, like with the rebels, is there any increase in sorcery then?

A: Oh, yes, in times like that it increases very much. They use it to overcome enemies, and they use it to hide themselves from their enemies.

Q: Does the user of sorcery want to overcome the enemy in the sense of killing them or just gaining power over them?

A: Certainly to kill them. There would be no use of sorcery to just catch the enemy, but always to kill. The sorcerer would have need to kill a person and change them to become something he could "play" with or use. You will read more about that in the material about Mukalay wa Ngoi.

Q: Are all deaths considered to be the result of sorcery?

A: Again I refer you to Mukalay wa Ngoi, but basically for all Africans, we believe that every death is caused by someone. We say that God does not kill anyone, only sorcery kills.

Q: Then must all deaths be avenged?

A: Absolutely, all deaths must be avenged. This brings so very much tragedy and difficult situations among us. There are, then, many people who are diviners who can point out the source of the sorcery that killed.

Q: Does the power of a sorcerer increase over the years?

A: Yes, definitely, because more and more "medicines" are added over the years, and this increases his possibilities. They start slowly in little things and then increase.

Q: In East Africa they say that the power of sorcery can actually be seen passing by in the night. Can the Aruund see this power?

A: No, it is invisible. No one can see it excepting the person to whom it was sent, that is the victim himself. Even the sorcerer himself cannot see it going.

Q: In East Africa if a person is afraid of sorcery passing by, or after seeing it go by, they take a piece of charcoal and throw it under the bed, and that takes care of the problem. Do the Aruund do this?

A: Now that you mention it, our elders told us that if we are afraid to sleep in a house alone, then we are to take charcoal and mark across our feet with it, or in some instances we were told to put it under our head and sleep with it there, at the head of the bed.

Q: Is there a difference between the slow illness or slow death and a quick sudden death?

A: No, not at all. It doesn't matter how quickly one dies, death is always caused by sorcery by some person.

Q: If I am afraid of sorcery, and if I want to get help from an anti-sorcery person, how does that work?

A: Yes, the anti-sorcery person is available to help. But if a person does not want to get involved in such things then that person is left in fear, without defense. If a person wants anti-sorcery, there are two kinds. There is a rather innocent kind that is to cancel out power of evil against them. There is another kind that does that through a rather reverse-curse, and evil is returned for evil.

Q: In other parts of Africa some people use a chicken to determine the guilt or innocence of suspected sorcerers. Do the Aruund use them too?

A: Almost all "medicines" that are made involve the use of a chicken; "medicines" to kill, and "medicines" to heal, and even the divining "medicine", all of these involve the use of a chicken. The diviners say, "A chicken is an animal which one must watch out for and beware of, for a chicken is able to discern the secrets of a man's heart." We use chickens to kill men and to heal men, for it has blood like a man.

Q: As concerns the power of anti-sorcery, can a mistake be made and that power kill the one who made it with the intent to kill another?

A: Oh, definitely. They often kill themselves. If they break one of the rules, or if they attempt to kill an innocent person, then their own sorcery can come back and kill them.

Q: Will sorcerers admit that they are, in fact, sorcerers?

A: Not all of them. On occasion, sorcerers will admit their sorceries if they have made a wrong accusation. Many, however, will never admit that they are sorcerers, especially if they do not have any palaver (trouble) with another person.

Q: Can a sorcerer kill a person of higher social standing than he, that is, can a commoner kill a chief?

A: Yes, certainly. Especially if the commoner wants the place of chief.

Q: What about the dreams of people, are they considered to be sorcery?

A: Dreams are always, or most always, seen in sleep, but a few are seen while waking. These do often reveal sorcery. There is fear in dreams in repetition. If the same dream comes several nights in a row, or if the same dream is dreamed twice in the same night, then there is great fear. Ordinary dreams, however, are not frightening. There are good dreams and bad dreams for us.

Q: What about a sorcerer who is converted to Christ, or who wants to be converted, do they have any difficulty being forgiven?

A: No, there is no problem, if the person truly comes clean and confesses everthing openly. Even though there is no problem with forgiveness like that, the people will follow that person (not follow him physically) in order to observe him. He will be under severe scrutiny. He can flee the sin of sorcery the same as any other sin.

APPENDIX V

Interview with Dr. Mbuya Katenga
LaPort, Indiana, November 10, 1979
Edited by Marvin S. Wolford

Basic information: Dr. K. Mbuya arrived at Samuteb (Piper) Memorial Hospital in December 1976 to become the first Zairian medical doctor to serve in that United Methodist institution. He is from the Baluba tribe near Kamina in North Shaba, and is the son of a United Methodist pastor. His training has been mostly in Kinshasa, Zaire (now Congo), and in 1979 he studied with three medical doctors in the USA. His interest in leading Bible studies while in medical school and his subsequent spiritual leadership have marked him as an outstanding man of faith. Some of his insights are recorded in this interview.

Q: As a medical doctor, what evidences do you see of sorcery in these days at Kapanga?

A: The people there tell me that when I go away from the hospital (for a trip) the patients also leave. Then when I return again, the patients also return. Therefore, they say that I have sorcery power. But I answer them and say that this is not true, "The patients come to the hospital because they know that I will treat them. When I am not here, they know that the nurses and Dr. Chambers will be treating only the children and the T.B. patients. When I am gone, she does not treat the other cases. . . that is why the patients come when I am here." But, the people don't believe that. They still believe that I have other power.

Q: What are specific examples of sorcery belief that you have witnessed at Kapanga?

A: One thing is that the people say they hear Dr. Eschtruth (murdered by rebels in 1977) working, and they hear him moving about in his house at night. I tell them that it is not true. I live in his house and even sleep in his bed, and he is not there, nor does he come in the night. They also say that there is a light on in my house (the late doctor's house) all night, and they think that the light is his spirit. But I tell them that I can assure them that no light is there.

Q: What evidence do you see at the hospital of people afraid of sorcery?

A: I do know that for we doctors (and I tell this to the other doctors who have come to work now at Kapanga) every word which we pronounce to the people is important. But doctors are like other people, and we like to joke with patients and say something like, "Oh, you have some sickness from your ancestors." But that is not good. You cannot do this kind of joking. It is very bad, because the patient will believe you.

Q: What can you say about the sorcery among the "Christians?" I say "Christians" realizing that as Mwant Yav Muteb said prior to his death, "There are but very few Christians in the true sense."

A: Truly, I can say now that this is very true. I noticed this first when I came to Kapanga at the time of a death. I saw everyone doing exactly the same things as the people who make no profession of faith. I even watched the wives of the pastors put whitewash on themselves just like the non-believers and I asked myself, "What is going on here?" When I asked one of them about it, she said, "Forgive me, doctor, I have not been able to bathe because we are mourning a death." I was very surprised, for that mother is a truly converted Christian. This was done to keep the dead spirit from coming near.

Q: Is it a problem of teaching from the Bible, and of knowing the Christian beliefs?

A: Yes, because to her, to put on the whitewash and to not bathe was not a wrong thing to do. I believe she did not really know the difference in a Christian behavior and a non-Christian one. They understand the big things, such as not killing and not drinking and not committing adultery, but to be afraid of a deceased person's spirit is just natural as far as they are concerned. It is not as if they do not yet know Jesus Christ as Saviour.

It is as you say, there is not adequate Christian education which deals with these things.

Q: You are a man who has traveled much in Zaire in recent years, in cities and in the bush, too. Do you see that sorcery is increasing or decreasing as compared to the times before Christianity came? (Perhaps before the turn of the century.)

A: In the past, before Christianity, we had sorcery, and then it was the normal thing, the ordinary thing. Everyone knew that fetishes were a normal part of life. Then, after, when our fathers began the work of pastors, people began to come out from those beliefs from the past. But what I see in this time, in these days, many people are returning to the fetishes and to sorcery, because many of the so-called Christians just don't know and understand about the Bible truths. The Bible is now regarded as a book, just as the books about chemistry or history. It is read as something relating to someone else only. It isn't seen in its true value.

Q: In some cases, it is said that sorcery increases because of uncertainties and because of war. Do you believe that this has happened in these war years now?

A: Well, I'm not so sure about that. Just now in Kolwezi, for example, the churches are filled with people, because they say plainly that death is not far away, in fact, it is very near. In May of 1978 we had war there, and the churches began to overflow, so they began two services each time they met. After one year and four months, they were still having attendance at that level. In that case, war pushed them into the church and warned them.

SOURCES CONSULTED

BOOKS

Allen, R. Earl. *The Hereafter.* Old Tappan: Fleming H. Revell Co., 1977.

Barrett, David B. *Schism and Renewal in Africa.* London: Oxford University Press, 1968.

Campbell, Dugald. *In the Heart of Bantuland.* Philadelphia: J. B. Lippincott Co., 1922.

Coleman, Robert E. *The Master Plan of Evangelism.* Old Tappan: Fleming H. Revell Co., 1963.

_____. *The Mind of the Master.* Old Tappan: Fleming H. Revell Co., 1973.

Cox, Leo George. *John Wesley's Concept of Perfection.* Kansas City: Beacon Hill Press of Kansas City, 1964.

Davidson, Basil. *The Africans.* London: Longman's, Green, & Co., 1969.

DeHaan, Richard W. and Lugt, Herbert Vander. *Satan, Satanism and Witchcraft.* Grand Rapids: Zondervan Publishing House, 1972.

Desai, Ram. *Christianity in Africa as Seen by Africans.* Denver: Alan Swallow, 1962.

Deschamps, Hubert. *Les Religions de L'Afrique Noire.* Paris: Presses Universitaires de France, 1965.

Dickson, Kwesi A. and Ellingworth, eds. *Biblical Revelation and African Beliefs.* Maryknoll: Orbis Books, 1969.

Engel, James F. *How Can I Get Them to Listen?* Grand Rapids: Zondervan Publishing House, 1977.

Engel, James F. and Norton H. Wilbert. *What's Gone Wrong with the Harvest?* Grand Rapids: Zondervan Publishing House, 1975.

Evans-Pritchard, E. E. *Witchcraft, Oracles, and Magic Among the Azande.* Abridged by Eva Gillies. London: Clarendon Press, Oxford, 1976.

Fisher, W. Singleton, and Hoyte, Julian. *Africa Looks Ahead.* London: Pickering & Inglis, 1948.

Fortes, Meyer. *Oedipus and Job in West African Religion.* Cambridge: At the University Press, 1959.

Fortes, M. and Dieterlan, G. *African Systems of Thought.* London: Oxford University Press, Reprinted 1972.

Gluckman, Max. *Custom and Conflict in Africa.* Oxford: Basil Blackwell, 1966.

Haliburton, Gordon MacKay. *The Prophet Harris.* London: Oxford University Press, 1973.

Hall, Edward T. *Beyond Culture.* Garden City: Anchor Press/ Doubleday; Anchor Books ed., Garden City: Anchor Press, 1977.

Harris, W. T., and Parrinder, E. G. *The Christian Approach to the Animist.* London: Edinburgh House Press, 1960.

Hastings, Adrian. *A History of African Christianity 1950-1975.* Cambridge: Cambridge University Press, 1979.

Hesselgrave, David J. *Communicating Christ Cross-Culturally.* Grand Rapids: Zondervan Publishing House, 1978.

_____. ed. *Theology and Mission.* Grand Rapids: Baker Book House, 1978.

Idowu, E. Bolaji. *African Traditional Religion*. Maryknoll: Orbis Books, 1975.

Johnston, Arthur P. *The Battle for World Evangelism*. Wheaton: Tyndale Publishers, 1978.

_____. *World Evangelism and The Word of God*. Minneapolis: Bethany Fellowship, 1974.

Jules-Rosette, Bennetta, ed. *The New Religions of Africa*. Norwood: Ablex Publishing Corp., 1979.

Kane, J. Herbert. *Christian Missions in Biblical Perspective*. Grand Rapids: Baker Book House, 1976.

Kato, Byang H. *Theological Pitfalls in Africa*. Kisumu, Kenya: Evangel Publishing House, 1975.

McFall, Ernest A. *Approaching the Nuer of Africa Through the Old Testament*. South Pasadena: William Carey Library, 1970.

McGavran, Donald. *The Clash Between Christianity and Cultures*. Washington, D. C.: Canon Press, 1974.

_____. *Understanding Church Growth*. Grand Rapids: William B. Eerdmans Publishing Co., 1970.

Mair, Lucy. *Witchcraft*. New York: McGraw-Hill Book Co., 1969.

Malinowski, Bronislaw. *The Dynamics of Culture Change*. New Haven: Yale University Press, 1961.

_____. *Magic, Science and Religion*. New York: Doubleday & Co., 1954.

Maquet, Jacques. *Power and Society in Africa*. Translated by Jeannette Kupfermann. New York: McGraw-Hill Book Co., 1971.

Marks, Isaac M. *Living With Fear.* New York: McGraw-Hill Book Co., 1978.

Martin, Marie-Louise. *Kimbangu.* Translated by D. M. Moore. Grand Rapids: William B. Eerdmans Publishing Co., 1975.

May, Rollo. *The Meaning of Anxiety.* New York: The Ronald Press Co., 1950.

Mayers, Marvin K. *Christianity Confronts Culture.* Grand Rapids: Zondervan Publishing House, 1974.

Mbiti, John S. *African Religions and Philosophy.* New York: Praeger Publishers, 1969; Anchor Books, 1970.

_____. *Concepts of God in Africa.* New York: Praeger Publishers, 1970.

_____. *Introduction to African Religion.* New York: Praeger Publishers, 1975.

_____. *New Testament Eschatology in an African Background.* London: Oxford University Press, 1971.

Merriam, Alan P. *Congo, Background of Conflict.* Evanston: Northwestern University Press, 1961.

Middleton, John, and Winter, E. H. *Foreword to Witchcraft and Sorcery in East Africa.* Edited by John Middleton and E. H. Winter. London: Routledge & Kegan Paul, 1963.

Nida, Eugene A. *Customs and Culture.* New York: Harper & Row Publishers, 1954.

_____. *Message and Mission.* South Pasadena: William Carey Library, 1975.

_____. *On Language, Culture and Religion.* The Hague: Mouton, 1974.

Nida, Eugene A., and Smalley, William A. *Introducing Animism.* New York: Friendship Press, 1959.

Okwuosa, V. E. Akubueze. *In the Name of Christianity.* Philadelphia: Dorrance & Co., 1977.

Oosterwal, Gottfried. *Modern Messianic Movements.* Elkhart: Institute of Mennonite Studies, 1973.

Oosthuizen, G. C. *Post Christianity in Africa.* Grand Rapids: William B. Eerdmans Publishing Co., 1968.

_____. *Theological Battleground in Asia and Africa.* New York: Humanities Press, 1972.

Packer, J. I. *Fundamentalism and The Word of God.* Grand Rapids: Eerdmans, 1978.

_____. *Knowing God.* Downers Grove: InterVarsity Press, 1973.

Parrinder, Geoffrey. *African Traditional Religion.* London: S.P.C.K., 1968.

_____. *West African Psychology.* London: Lutterworth Press, 1951. Reprint Edition, New York: AMS Press, 1976.

Pentecost, J. Dwight. *Your Adversary The Devil.* Grand Rapids: Zondervan Publishing House, 1969.

Peters, George W. *A Biblical Theology of Missions.* Chicago: Moody Press, 1972.

_____. *Saturation Evangelism.* Grand Rapids: Zondervan Publishing House, 1970.

Pfister, Oscar. *Christianity and Fear.* Translated by W. H. Johnston. London: George Allen and Unwin, 1948.

Phillips, Godfrey E. *The Transmission of Faith*. London: Lutterworth Press, 1946.

Ravensdale, Tom, and Morgan, James. *The Psychology of Witchcraft*. New York: Arco Publishing Co., 1974.

Ray, Benjamin C. *African Religions*. Englewood Cliffs: Prentice-Hall, 1976.

Reid, Alexander. *The Roots of Lomomba: Mongo Land*. Hicksville: Exposition Press, 1979.

Reynolds, Barrie. *Magic, Divination and Witchcraft Among the Barotse of Northern Rhodesia*. Berkeley: University of California Press, 1963.

Seaver, George. *David Livingstone: His Life and Letters*. New York: Harper and Brothers Publishers, 1957.

Smith, Edwin W. *African Beliefs and Christian Faith*. London: The United Society for Christian Literature, 1936.

_____. *The Shrine of a People's Soul*. New York: Friendship Press, 1947.

Smith, Edwin W. and Dale, Andrew Murray. *The Ila-Speaking Peoples of Northern Rhodesia*. 2 vols. New Hyde Park: University Books, 1968.

Stock, Frederick and Margaret. *People Movements in the Punjab*. South Pasadena: William Carey Library, 1975.

Stonelake, Alfred R. *Congo, Past and Present*. London: World Dominion Press, 1937.

Summers, Montague. *Witchcraft and Black Magic*. New York: Causeway Books, 1974.

Sundkler, Bengt. *The Christian Ministry in Africa*. London: SCM Press, 1962.

Tippett, Alan R. *The Deep Sea Canoe*. South Pasadena: William Carey Library, 1977.

_____. *People Movements in Southern Polynesia*. Chicago: Moody Press, 1971.

_____. *Peoples of Southwest Ethiopia*. South Pasadena: William Carey Library, 1970.

Visser 'T Hooft, W. A. *No Other Name*. Philadelphia: The Westminster Press, 1963.

Westermann, Diedrich. *Africa and Christianity*. London: Oxford University Press, 1937.

White, John Wesley. *The Devil*. Wheaton: Tyndale House Publishers, 1977.

Wiley, H. Orton. *Christian Theology*. 3 vols. Kansas City: Beacon Hill Press of Kansas City, 1940, 1952, 1953.

Wilson, Monica. *Religion and the Transformation of Society*. Cambridge: At the University Press, 1971.

Wynkoop, Mildred Bangs. *Wesleyan-Arminian Theology*. Kansas City: Beacon Hill Press of Kansas City, 1967.

ARTICLES IN BOOKS

Allott, Antony. "The African Conception of the Rule of Law." In *Development: For What?*, pp. 75-102. Edited by John H. Hallowell. Durham: Duke University Press, 1964.

Beattie, John. "Sorcery in Bunyoro." In *Witchcraft and Sorcery in East Africa*, pp. 27-56. Edited by John Middleton and E. H. Winter. London: Routledge & Kegan Paul, 1963.

Beyerhaus, Peter. "Mission Humanization and the Kingdom." In *Crucial Issues in Missions Tomorrow*, pp. 54-76. Edited by Donald A. McGavran. Chicago: Moody Bible Institute, 1972.

Bryan, G. McLeod. "Religious Developments in Africa." In *Development: For What?*, pp. 182-212. Edited by John H. Hallowell. Durham: Duke University Press, 1964.

Douglas, Mary. "The Lele of Kasai." In *African Worlds*, pp. 1-27. Edited by Daryll Forde. London: Oxford University Press, 1954.

Doutreloux, M. A. "Prophetisme et Culture." In *African Systems of Thought*, pp. 224-239. Edited by M. Fortes and G. Dieterlan. London: Oxford University Press, 1965.

Fortes, Meyer. "Some Reflections on Ancestor Worship in Africa." In *African Systems of Thought*, pp. 122-144. Edited by M. Fortes and G. Dieterlan. London: Oxford University Press, 1965.

Hardyman, Marjorie. "The Church and Sorcery in Madagascar." In *African Initiatives in Religion*, pp. 208-221. Edited by David B. Barrett. Nairobi: East African Publishing House, 1971.

Hulstaert, Pere G. "La Sorcellerie Chez Les Mongo." In *African Systems of Thought*, pp. 165-170. Edited by M. Fortes and G. Dieterlan. London: Oxford University Press, 1965.

Kwast, Lloyd. "Christianity and Culture: Biblical Bedrock." In *Crucial Issues in Missions Tomorrow*, pp. 159-174. Edited by Donald A. McGavran. Chicago: Moody Bible Institute, 1972.

LaFonatine, Jean. "Witchcraft in Bugisu." In *Witchcraft and Sorcery in East Africa*, pp. 187-220. Edited by John Middleton and E. H. Winter. London: Routledge & Kegan Paul, 1963.

Marwick, M. G. "Some Problems in the Sociology of Sorcery and Witchcraft." In *African Systems of Thought*, pp. 171-191. Edited by M. Fortes and G. Dieterlan. London: Oxford University Press, 1965.

Mbiti, John S. "Christ and the Younger Churches." In *Christ and the Younger Churches*, pp. 51-62. Edited by Georg F. Vicedom. London: S.P.C.K., 1972.

_____. "Christianity and Traditional Religions in Africa." In *Crucial Issues in Missions Tomorrow*, pp. 144-158. Edited by Donald A. McGavran. Chicago: Moody Bible Institute, 1972.

_____. "Some African Concepts of Christology." In *Christ and the Younger Churches*, pp. 51-62. Edited by Georg F. Vicedom. London: S.P.C.K., 1972.

McGavran, Donald A. "The Mandala Mission Field." In *Church Growth and Group Conversion*, pp. 36-48. Edited by Donald A. McGavran. Pasadena: William Carey Library, 1973.

_____. "When the Church Grows." In *Church Growth and Group Conversion*, pp. 97-116. Edited by Donald A. McGavran. Pasadena: William Carey Library, 1973.

Ojike, Mbonu. "Christianity in Africa." In *Christianity as Seen by Africans*, pp. 60-67. Edited by Ram Desai. Denver: Alan Swallow, 1962.

Pickett, J. W. "Possibility of Ingathering at Dhamtari." In *Church Growth and Group Conversion*, pp. 61-70. Edited by Donald A. McGavran. Pasadena: William Carey Library, 1973.

_____. "Satnami People Movements." In *Church Growth and Group Conversion*, pp. 84-96. Edited by Donald A. McGavran. Pasadena: William Carey Library, 1973.

Shuenemann, Detmar. "Evangelization Among Occultists and Spiritists." In *Let the Earth Hear His Voice*, pp. 885-894. Edited by J. D. Douglas. Minneapolis: World Wide Publications, 1975.

Steere, Douglas V. "Development: For What?" In *Development: For What?*, pp. 213-234. Edited by John H. Hallowell. Durham: Duke University Press, 1964.

Tippett, Alan R. "The Evangelization of Animists." In *Let the Earth Hear His Voice*, pp. 844-855. Edited by J. D. Douglas. Minneapolis: World Wide Publications, 1975.

_____. "The Holy Spirit and Responsive Populations." In *Crucial Issues in Missions Tomorrow*, pp. 77-101. Edited by Donald A. McGavran. Chicago: Moody Bible Institute, 1972.

_____. "Possessing the Philosophy of Animism for Christ." In *Crucial Issues in Missions Tomorrow*, pp. 125-143. Edited by Donald A. McGavran. Chicago: Moody Bible Institute, 1972.

Winter, E. H. "The Enemy Within: Amba Witchcraft." In *Witchcraft and Sorcery in East Africa*, pp. 277-299. Edited by John Middleton and E. H. Winter. London: Routledge & Kegan Paul, 1963.

ARTICLES IN PERIODICALS

Adeney, Miriam Ann. "What is 'Natural' About Witchcraft and Sorcery?" *Missiology* 2 (July 1974): 377-395.

DeRidder, Richard R. "God and the Gods: Reviewing the Biblical Roots." *Missiology* 6 (January 1978): 11-28.

Fehderau, Harold W. "Kimbanguism: Prophetic Christianity in Congo." *Practical Anthropology* 9 (July-August 1962): 159, 162.

McGavran, Donald A. "God's Royal Power in Zaire: An Evaluation of the State of the Church." *Missiology* 6 (January 1978): 81-90.

Martin, Marie-Louise. "Confessing Christ in the Kimbanguist Church." *International Review of Mission* 64 (January 1975): 25-29.

Nacpil, Emerito P. "Theological Education in a Changing Society." *The South East Asia Journal of Theology* 9 (April 1968): 17-35.

REFERENCE BOOKS

Clarke's Commentary, Abingdon reprint ed. S.v. "I Samuel," by Adam Clarke.

Nave's Topical Bible, reprint ed. (1977).

The New International Dictionary of New Testament Theology, 1st English ed., (1976). S.v. "Magic," Colin Brown, and J. Stafford Wright.

Webster's New World Dictionary, 2nd college ed. S.v. "Animism."

The Wesleyan Commentary, 1st ed. S.v. "Ezekiel," by Bert Harold Hall.

INTERVIEWS

Mbuya, Katenga. Congolese medical doctor, formerly at Samuteb (Piper) Memorial Hospital, Kapanga, Shaba Province, Zaire (now Congo). Interview November 10, 1979. D. Miss. major project, Trinity Evangelical Divinity School, 1981. Marvin S. Wolford.

Sampas, Nshid. Ordained minister, United Methodist Church, Southern Congo Annual Conference. Interviews, January 27, 1979; January 29, 1979; February 8, 1979; February 19, 1979. D. Miss. major project, Trinity Evangelical Divinity School, 1981. Marvin S. Wolford.

Wakadilo, Ngoi (now deceased). Bishop, United Methodist Church, North Shaba Annual Conference, Zaire (now Republic of Congo). Interview, May 29, 1979. D. Miss. major project, Trinity Evangelical Divinity School, 1981. Marvin S. Wolford.

MESSAGE

Ngoi, Mukalay wa. "Sorcery for Killing." English translation of transcript of message given at Mulungwishi Methodist Seminary, Southern Zaire(now Congo), 1975. D. Miss. major project, Trinity Evangelical Divinity School, 1981. Marvin S. Wolford.

THESES

Hoover, J. Jeffrey. "The Seduction of Ruwej: Reconstructing Ruund History." Ph.D. dissertation, Yale University, 1978.

Harvey, William R. Research notes taken at the Musée d' Afrique Centrale (Brussels, Belgium) concerning history of Lunda people, Democratic Republic of Congo.